The Craftsman's Art Series

The Craft of
Knitting

Rae Compton

Stanley Paul, London

Stanley Paul & Co Ltd
3 Fitzroy Square, London W1

An imprint of the Hutchinson Publishing Group

London Melbourne Sydney Auckland
Wellington Johannesburg and agencies
throughout the world

First published 1976
© Rae Compton 1976
Illustrations © Stanley Paul & Co Ltd 1976

Printed in Great Britain by litho by The Anchor Press Ltd
and bound by Wm Brendon & Son Ltd, both of
Tiptree, Essex

ISBN 0 09 124810 8 (cased)
      0 09 124811 6 (paperback)

Contents

Acknowledgements

Miss Stewart of Highland Home Industries, 90 George Street, Edinburgh, for the modern Fairisle and for the photograph of the ring shawl.

Mr Richard Robson, Curator of the Castle Howard costume gallery, for lending the nineteenth-century book for photography.

Mr Peter Stirling for his photograph taken at Castle Howard.

The London Museum for permission to publish the photograph of the shirt worn by Charles I.

1. The Creative Craft

Few crafts, if any, offer as much variety and scope for the individual as knitting. It can be suited to your capabilities and to your age-group, to what you want to make and to the amount you can afford to spend on materials. Good results can be produced immediately you have mastered and practised the very simplest stitches, and if you want to explore the fascination of how stitches can be used to create patterns and texture interest, how shaping can be best used and even how to design for yourself, the possibilities are endless.

The equipment you need is inexpensive and can be assembled gradually so that there need be no great expense to meet before you can get down to work. Also there is no storage problem or 'wherever can I find room to work' question to be solved before you can begin. There is a constant supply of new ideas in leaflets, magazines and books, with detailed working instructions for not only garments for all the family, but home furnishings, accessories for yourself and home, and ideas for gifts and bazaar items.

Knitting is too often associated with armchairs. It is not simply a craft to occupy your fingers while you are being entertained by television. It is a creative craft with a long and interesting history, a craft that has been carried world-wide and has its roots very far back in the past.

When in 1527 the Paris Guild was set up with St Fiacre as its patron saint, to maintain the high standard that the craft had reached, an apprentice had to spend three years learning the craft. After three years he travelled abroad to study the progress being made and techniques used by other craftsmen. Only then was he considered to be experienced enough to sit an examination which lasted over several weeks, terminating in his making of a test piece which was a fine knitted carpet depicting flowers and birds and intertwined leaves, which he must state was entirely original and not copied in any way. This was no small piece of work, for it had to measure 10 feet by 8 feet.

But knitting began long before this. A tiny doll's cap, not more than 2 inches long, found at Bahnasa in Egypt, would seem to establish that knitting was well known by as early as 1000 BC, although it was rather laboriously produced on frames not unlike the cotton reels or 'knitting nancies' of our times.

Knitting on needles as we know it today may well have been known by the time of Christ, for a knitted doll has been found that has been dated at about the time of Cleopatra.

This book is intended for all those who would like to learn to knit, and also for those who may never have made very much progress.

The beginner is taken slowly and in detail, with the help of diagrams, through the steps required to produce knitting. Once the early techniques have been learned and put into practice, many of the other methods of producing shape and pattern are explained.

It is hoped that any knitter working through these steps will find that they are able, with ease, to select work they will enjoy carrying out.

For the knitter who wants to know more, details are given about how to start making your own designs and a list has been compiled that will help you to extend your knowledge further with the help of other books.

There need be no limit to what you knit or even with what you knit, for like all crafts there is always room for experiment and some of the most creative ideas are as yet unworked. At a time when many new forms are being developed you may like to see what you can make using unusual 'yarns': string, ribbon, strips of material and cords are all knittable and for decorative wall hangings have many possibilities.

One word about knitting machines versus hand knitting. Many people feel that machine knitting is simply a much quicker way of producing knitting. It is certainly quicker but should be treated as a craft on its own. Stitches are made in the same way, by working rows of loops, but there the likeness should be allowed to end. By all means experiment with machine knitting as well as hand knitting, but try to keep them apart. To get the best from both crafts they should not be constantly compared but each should be treated and considered on its own merits and as a separate type of creative activity.

2. Equipment

Simple, cheap equipment will serve even the most experienced knitter.

Some things are useful right from the start, and can be collected together before you go any further.

A Place to Keep your Work

A capacious work bag or box is essential for keeping both the work you are actually doing and the small things you will need from time to time.

Begin as you mean to go on and make certain that those around you know that it is your bag or box. Be firm, then you won't find the contents wandering off to the playroom or even the potting shed.

Once you start to make pieces of knitting that have to be folded up between knitting sessions, it is a good idea to have an additional clean cloth or napkin or a polythene bag to wrap it in. This will help to keep it clean and fresh until it is finished.

Add the following items to your box and you will be ready to begin.

A small, sharp-pointed pair of scissors.
A 12 inch ruler.
A strong tape measure – not made of paper.
A card of blunt-ended wool needles.
A pencil and small notebook.
One large and one small stitchholder.

Beginners

In this chapter you will find information about yarn, needles and further equipment. It is important that you take time to read it, otherwise you will find that later on you will come across something that seems to make no sense at all.

Needles

For yarn that has been suggested you will need one pair of knitting needles, size No. 8.

Knitting needles are available in three different lengths. The only way to find out which length you prefer is to try them and see.

Your choice may be influenced by the knitters you already know. Because I come from the north I always use 14 inch needles and feel very lost if I can't tuck the end of the needle in my right hand under my right arm as I work.

The other two lengths are 10 and 12 inches.

Needles, because you use them all the time, are worth some extra thought. British sizes range from the very fine size 16 to thick needles such as size 1. There are fatter needles graded 0,00 and 000, but these are used only for thick or open work such as blanket and rug knitting.

The best needles are the ones that look the most uninteresting because, instead of being brightly coloured, they are plain grey. They are made from light metal which is treated in such a way that the metal on the outside forms a 'coat' which never harms the yarn.

The best-known makes are Aero and Milward Disc.

A good needle with the correct tip adds greatly to the comfort of knitting and also to the ease with which the needle slips into the stitch. Cheap needles can be very sharp, tend to split stitches, complicate the work, and are often sore on fingers. They also tend to break more readily.

A set of needles can last a very long time if they are looked after. If they are often bent out of shape and have to be straightened before use, the day will come when your even knitting becomes spoilt and irregular. When this happens it is time to replace them.

Pairs of needles for 'flat' knitting are pointed only at one end. 'Flat' knitting is the term given to pieces of knitting that are knitted in rows working backwards and forwards with a pair of needles.

Sets of needles are usually sold as four needles to a set in Britain and are pointed at both ends. They are used for knitting seamless articles in the 'round' as for instance in many glove, mitten and sock patterns (see page 58).

A circular needle which is easily bent and is tipped by two needle points can be used in place of a set of needles for larger seamless garments such as skirts and sweaters (see page 59).

Other Equipment

A rotary row counter will help you to keep check of the number of rows you have worked and you will also find *a needle gauge* may be of use so that you can check needle sizes if you are in doubt.

Equipment Needed for Pressing

Before you have gone very far you will want to press the stitches. For this you will need:

A box of rustless steel pins

An ironing pad   The surface that you use for ironing may well be sufficiently padded. If not, it is essential to make a thick pad from several thicknesses of blanket stitched together. Tapes at the corners can secure it to the ironing table legs.

Cotton pressing cloths   These are best made from white or un-bleached cotton which avoids the possibility of the colour staining the yarn.

Yarns

What Yarn Means

Yarn is the name given to all types of threads that you may use in a lifetime of knitting. They are made of a wide variety of different raw materials (see below). This can be confusing, so, for learning, buy just a few balls of plain double knitting wool in a colour that you like and a shade that is not too dark or too pale.

It is better to use new yarn than to practise with odd left-over ends. These may be crumpled and make it difficult for you to see the stitches and patterns. Wendy and Sirdar both make a good double knitting yarn that is firmly spun and ideal for beginning.

Natural Yarns

Natural yarns are those that come from plants or animals or, as in the case of silk, are made by an insect.

Wool, from sheep-fleece, is one of the most useful of all yarns. Goats are the source of mohair, and angora is the fine fluffy yarn made from angora rabbits' fur.

Cotton and linen come from plants, and cotton in particular is used a great deal in hand knitting.

Man-made Fibres

These are produced from chemicals. Fine threads are then spun into suitable yarn for knitting. Nylon is one of the best known of these yarns, but the group includes other names such as terylene, courtelle, acrilan, and orlon.

Experiments are continually being carried out on these yarns and many man-made fibres today have more of the qualities of natural fibres which in their early days they lacked. The subject of yarns is dealt with at a greater length in chapter 10.

It is important to consider thickness. Too many people think that one 4 ply yarn must automatically be the same as any other. This is not the case. The ply does not indicate thickness, but only how many threads have been spun together to make it. Double knitting yarn is a perfect example of this because it is very often spun from four threads but is also usually nearly twice as thick as a 4 ply yarn. Even to this there are exceptions.

Most knitting instructions state quite clearly what yarn to use for any given design. It is always better to use this, but there are times when it may be impossible to obtain. Only in this case is it advisable to substitute one yarn for another.

Because it is quite a specialized job to substitute correctly, this will be dealt with later in the book where detailed information will be given.

A chart has also been included so that you may see at a glance which yarns may be expected to knit to similar tensions and there-fore be successful in substitution.

3. Beginnings

All knitting starts with a slip knot.

Fold the yarn into a loop exactly as shown in the diagram.

Pick the loop up in your left hand without disturbing it and draw a double loop of the yarn from beyond the first loop towards the ball through the first loop.

Take one knitting needle and slip the new loop on to it and draw it up, so that it does not slip off the needle too easily.

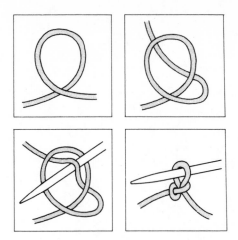

The four stages of making a slip knot.

This slip knot is used as a starting stitch. Making other stitches is called 'casting on'.

There are several different methods of casting on, each of which has its own special purpose.

The two-needle method which we use here (sometimes called the English Cable method) is a good, all-purpose, strong cast-on edge.

Two-needle Casting On

This method uses both of a pair of needles.

Already you have placed the slip knot on one needle. Put the needle with the slip knot into your left hand.

Take the other needle in your right hand and insert the point of it into the loop on the left-hand needle, passing the tip from the front to the back of the stitch.

Bring the yarn end that is attached to the ball up round the point of the right-hand needle.

Using the right-hand needle, draw the loop made by the yarn through the original loop on the needle.

Place the new loop on to the left-hand needle so that you now have two loops on this needle.

*Insert the tip of the right-hand needle between the two loops on the left-hand needle, bring the yarn round the point just as when you were making the last stitch and draw a new loop through.

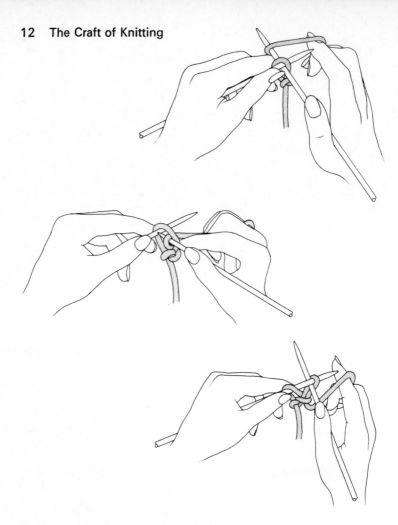

Casting on using the two needle method.

Place the new loop on to the left-hand needle so that there are now three stitches.

Continue in this way from where the asterisk mark * is until there are fifteen loops on the left-hand needle.

Now you have cast on fifteen stitches.

Stitches to become 'knitting' have to be worked backwards and forwards in rows, lengthening the loops on each row by the addition of another row immediately above them.

There are two ways in which stitches can be worked in their rows. They can be 'knitted' or 'purled'.

To Knit Stitches

Place the needle with the 'cast on' stitches in your left hand, and take the other needle in your right hand.

Insert the tip of the right-hand needle into the first stitch on the other needle, passing the tip of the needle through the stitch from the front to the back.

Bring the end of yarn attached to the ball up and round the tip of the right-hand needle and use the right-hand needle to draw this yarn through as a new loop.

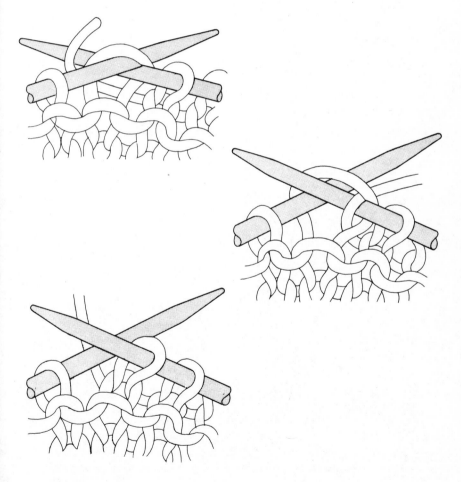

How to knit a stitch.

Once the loop is through, the stitch can be kept on the right-hand needle and the left-hand needle withdrawn from the old loop. Thus one stitch has been knitted.

Now knit the next stitch on the left-hand needle in just the same way, finishing with it on the right-hand needle.

Continue until all the stitches are on the right-hand needle.

Now you have knitted one row.

Change the needles over so that the stitches are in your left hand and work another row.

Continue in this way for several rows.

When you knit every row, the pattern it makes is called *garter stitch*.

To Purl Stitches

Purl stitches are made in a slightly different way, but it is just as simple.

Place the needle with the stitches in your left hand and the empty needle in the other hand.

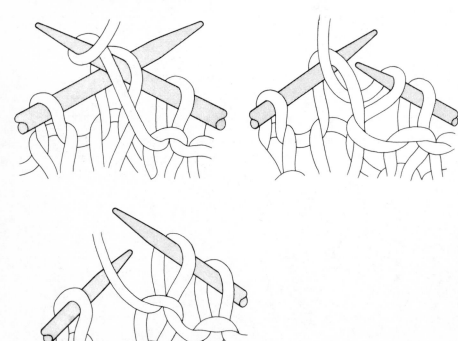

How to purl a stitch.

Left: Garter stitch.

Centre: Stocking stitch, smooth or plain side.

Right: Stocking stitch, purl or rough side.

Insert the right-hand needle tip into the first stitch on the left-hand needle passing the tip through the loop from back to front.

Bring the yarn up and round the needle point and use the right-hand needle to draw a new loop back through the original loop.

Once the new loop is on the right-hand needle withdraw the left-hand needle from the old loop. Now you have purled one stitch.

Purl the other stitches along the row in the same way.

Work several rows in this way, purling each row.

Look at the pattern these rows have made. You will see that it looks very like garter stitch, although it may not be quite so even.

Because most people do not purl quite as evenly as they knit, garter stitch is usually worked by knitting every row.

To Work Stocking Stitch

Before you learn how to finish a piece of work off, see what difference is made by knitting the next row and purling the row after that, and repeating this for several rows.

You will see that all the loops are formed on one side, called the purl or rough side, while the other side is plain or smooth. When the smooth side is used as the right or facing side of the finished fabric this combination is called 'stocking stitch', and reverse stocking stitch when the rough or purl side is used as the right side.

One more very important fact! In garter stitch you had the same number of loops on both sides of the fabric, first on one side and then on the other. This produces a fabric that lies flat and can therefore be used for edgings. If the stocking stitch section had been at the cast-on edge you would see how it curls up because all the loops are on one side of the fabric. Therefore, main sections of garments knitted in stocking or reverse stocking stitch must have edgings in garter stitch (or some other method of keeping them flat).

Holding the Yarn

The way you hold the yarn is a personal choice. Many people, however, begin by never trying to hold it in the way that could be called 'right'.

When it is allowed just to hang down as you work and is picked up separately for each stitch, the work is slow and you will never get an even flow. It is really worth while, however slow and odd it may feel for a little, to get used to wrapping it round your fingers, as the diagram shows. In this way it is controlled, and so to some extent it flows similarly for all the stitches, making for an even texture.

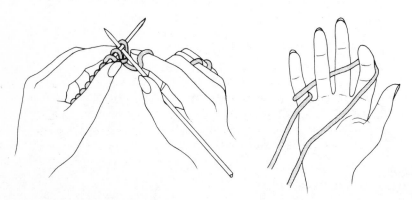

One way of holding the yarn.

The easiest way to hold it is round your smallest finger, between the next two fingers, and over the tip of your first finger which is used to guide it to just where you want it. Do practise. It soon becomes 'second nature' and you will be glad that you have spent the time learning.

Joining Yarn

Never, ever, join yarn in the middle of a row.

This harsh warning is seriously meant. More knitters fail tests as craftswomen by doing this than by any other one point.

Join a new ball at the beginning of a row. The long ends will be useful for making up, for sewing on buttons or strengthening the back of button positions.

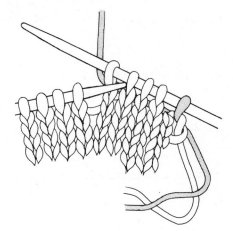

Joining in a new ball of yarn.

Beginning a New Ball

When the yarn is almost finished leave the end hanging at the start of a new row. Fold the end of the new ball into a loop with several inches hanging down. Loop the end over the needle for the first stitch and just carry on knitting with the new ball. When really long ends are left they are annoying as you continue to work, so cut them off and save them, leaving at least 6 inches for darning in. Too short an end can mean dropped stitches and a tedious taking-back and reworking session.

Assessing the Amount of Yarn for a Row

As a general principle allow four times the length of the row in yarn. As with every principle there are exceptions and some books state that three times the length is sufficient. There are certainly times when this is not so and it is better to be safe than sorry. The longer the row and thicker the yarn, the more likely you are to find that my rule is fair.

Yarn Joining Exceptions

Fairisle, Norwegian or jacquard-type patterns sometimes give a chance to join yarn in the middle of the row when a shade is being reintroduced to the pattern.

The method of joining is exactly the same as when it is joined at the end of the row, but of course it will mean extra ends to darn in on the wrong side when the work is complete.

The other exception is when you are working 'in the round' and there are no row ends (see page 61).

To Cast Off

Knitting is finished by being 'cast off'.

Knit the first two stitches of the next row.

Using the tip of the left-hand needle, lift the stitch furthest to the right on the right-hand needle over the stitch next to it, so that only one stitch remains on the right hand needle.

Knit one more stitch so that you again have two and lift one over the other as before.

Continue working all along the row until only one stitch remains on the right-hand needle.

Cut the yarn several inches towards the ball and draw the end through the last stitch.

It is possible to cast off stitches purlwise, purling the stitches instead of knitting them. When casting off, all stitches which are knit should be cast off knitwise, all purl stitches should be cast off purlwise.

Once you know how to purl and knit, and how to cast on and off, there is very little else that you can do to stitches. Don't think

Casting off   (a) lifting 1st stitch over the 2nd,
              (b) one stitch is cast off, knit the next following stitch.

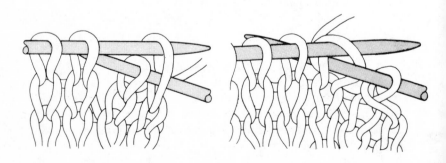

that knitting does not become more exciting. There is a lot to learn yet, but it is all built around these four processes.

Two more stitch procedures are vital and useful.

To Slip a Stitch

When patterns are being built up it may be necessary to slip a stitch from one needle to the other without working it.

There are two things that can be done with the yarn in cases like this.

Slipping a Stitch with the Yarn in Front

Bring the yarn round to the front of the work from the last stitch you worked.

Insert the tip of the right-hand needle into the stitch to be slipped as if you were going to purl it, that is from back to front, and pass it from the left to the right needle. Now you are ready to purl the next stitch, or to take the yarn back to the back of the work and knit the next stitch.

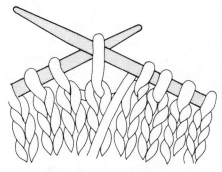

Slipping stitches with the yarn carried across the work as a decorative pattern.

When the yarn is carried across the front in this way it is usually used to build up a pattern.

Slipping a Stitch with the Yarn Behind

This could be called the 'hidden' method and is worked in exactly the same way, slipping the stitch as if it were to be purled, but keeping the yarn behind the stitch on the wrong side.

Unless a pattern specially tells you to slip a stitch knitwise, you

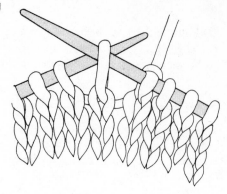

Slipping a stitch purlwise with the yarn passing behind the slipped stitch to the following stitch.

should always slip it purlwise, otherwise the stitches will have a twisted appearance when they are re-worked in the next row.

To Twist a Stitch

There are times when the smoothness of stocking stitch is slightly altered by inserting the needle into the back of the stitch. The remainder of the stitch is formed in the same way. When the knit row of stocking stitch is worked in this way it changes its name to 'continental' or 'twisted stocking stitch' and instead of saying we have knitted the stitch we call it knitting through the back of the loop. It is also possible to purl a stitch through the back of the loop. When both knit and purl rows are worked through the back of the loops a firmer and closer fabric is formed.

The Language of Knitting

The words used in describing knitting, and particularly in giving instructions for stitch patterns, are usually abbreviated.

Most abbreviations are standard but it is always best to check the list supplied with all instructions.

Already you have learned to knit, which is usually shortened to 'k' or 'K', and purl to 'p' or 'P'.

You can also slip a stitch, which is usually followed by the number of stitches to be slipped and will be either 'sl 1' or 'Sl 1'. If you are not to slip it purlwise then it may be written as 'Sl 1 knitwise'.

You have also worked into the back of knit and purl stitches which is called 'through the back' and may be written for one or more stitch as 'K1 tbl' or if it is a complete row – *1st row*   K, tbl.

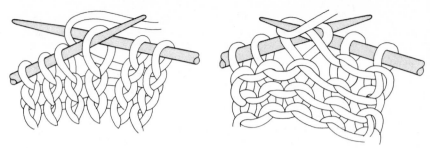

Knitting a stitch through the back of the loop.
Purling a stitch through the back of the loop.

If it is to work into the back of the loop of purl stitches it will be 'P1 tbl'.

Either the capital letter K, or the lower-case letter k is used and varied from leaflet to leaflet, but in this book we shall in future use the capital letter as the abbreviation.

4. Creating Shape

Shaping is a twofold process. It can be used to shape the piece of fabric or it can be used to create stitch interest and patterns.

To Increase

Increasing is creating extra stitches.

Simple Increasing

The simplest way of increasing is to knit twice into a stitch, whether it is knit or purl, making two stitches out of one.

When the stitch is to be made out of a knit stitch, work to the stitch and then insert the right-hand needle point from front to back into the stitch to be increased.

Bring the yarn round and over the point and draw through the new loop.

Before you slip the left-hand needle away, knit into the back of the loop still on the left-hand needle by bringing the yarn round

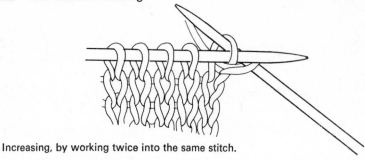

Increasing, by working twice into the same stitch.

the point and drawing through a new loop which will be on the right-hand needle.

When both new stitches are on the right-hand needle the other needle can be withdrawn and the rest of the row worked in the usual way.

Increasing a purl stitch is worked in the same manner. Purl the first loop in the usual way, but before slipping the left-hand needle out purl again into the back of the same loop that is still held open by the left-hand needle and then, with two new loops on the right-hand needle slip the other one out and complete the row.

The usual way of abbreviating this is simply to state 'increase' which is shortened to 'inc'. It is usually assumed that you can see whether the stitch is knit or purl.

It is often preferable to increase between two stitches and in this case the yarn between the two stitches is lifted on to the left-hand needle with the tip of the right-hand needle.

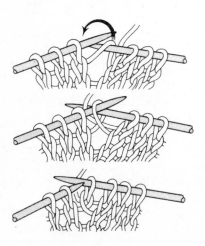

Increasing, by working a stitch between two stitches.

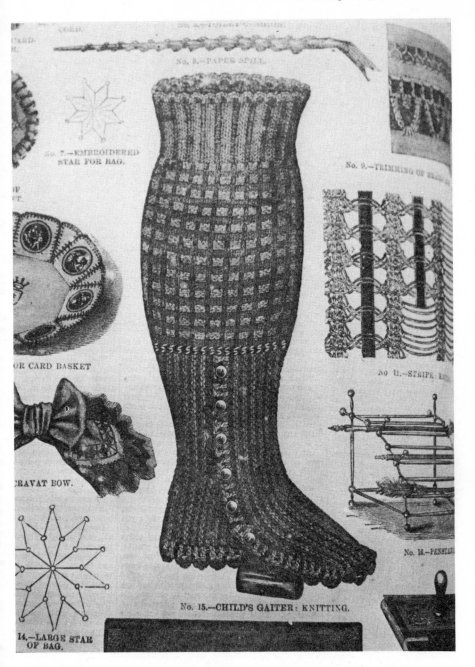

No. 8.—PAPER SPILL.

No. 7.—EMBROIDERED STAR FOR BAG.

No. 9.—TRIMMING OF

CARD BASKET

CRAVAT BOW.

No. 11.—STRIPE

No. 12.—PEN

No. 15.—CHILD'S GAITER: KNITTING.

14.—LARGE STAR OF BAG.

Page from a 19th century knitting book.

It is possible to increase a stitch by knitting this loop but it will leave a small space. The space is avoided by knitting or purling into the back of the loop that has been lifted. Alternatively, you could twist the loop once as you place it on the left-hand needle. If you twist it first, you must knit or purl it in the ordinary way, without working through the back of the loop.

This is called 'make 1' and is most often abbreviated to 'M1'. Where there might be doubt as to whether it should be knitted or purled the additional letter may be added 'M1K' or 'M1P'.

Invisible Increase

The increase which shows least is made by knitting into the stitch below the next stitch on the needle and then knitting into the stitch above it, thus again making two stitches where there was only one before.

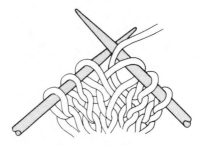

Working an invisible increase.

When you try this for yourself you will see that the made stitch tends to slope towards the right. When it is being used at either side of a sweater or sleeve, the increase at the right can be worked as described, but the one at the left should be worked in the opposite order. Work the stitch on the needle first and then knit into the loop below the stitch you have worked.

Now the increase will slope towards the left. This method of increasing is seldom used by designers in this country, although it is a favourite of mine. Because of this there is no standard abbreviation, although it could be easily called 'M1B' for 'make 1 below'. Although it is so seldom mentioned, you would do well to remember it and use it when the choice of method is left to you, or when you are designing garments for yourself.

Lace Increase

Increases do not always need to be invisible or hidden.

Often in pattern-making the increase is used to form the pattern itself. This is particularly so when you are working lace patterns.

In this case they are made by putting the yarn over the needle between two stitches and the new loop is not actually worked until the following row.

This increase, worked between two knit stitches, is made as follows:

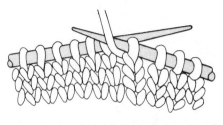

A lace increase between two knit stitches, yarn over needle.

Knit the first stitch. Before you knit another stitch, bring the yarn round to the front of the work and over the needle in readiness for knitting the next stitch.

This is called either 'yarn forward' or more correctly 'yarn over needle' and is abbreviated to 'yfd' or 'yfwd' or to 'yon'. 'Yon' is the abbreviation that will be used in this book.

When 'yfwd' is used it is because when you bring the yarn to the front and it is followed by a knit stitch you have to take it over the needle to get it into the correct position for the next stitch.

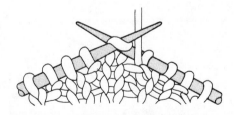

A lace increase between a purl and a knit stitch, yarn over needle.

When you are working this type of increase between a purl and a knit stitch the abbreviation would again be 'yon', because the yarn is forward when you finish the purl stitch. It has to be taken over the needle both to make a stitch and to have it in the correct position for the stitch to be knitted.

When a purl stitch follows a knit stitch the increase is called 'yarn round needle' because you have to bring it forward and over the needle and round to the front again ready for the purl stitch. The abbreviation is 'yrn'.

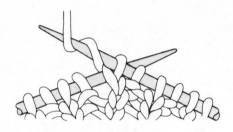

A lace increase between a knit and a purl stitch, yarn round needle.

Where it is worked between two purl stitches it is again 'yrn' because it has to be taken over the needle and back round to the front again in readiness for the following purl stitch.

Although it takes many words to describe, in practice it is simple to do.

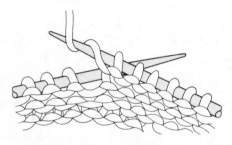

A lace increase between two purl stitches, yarn round needle.

To Decrease

Simple Decreasing

By far the most often used decrease is where two stitches are worked together into one stitch by knitting or purling through both stitches at the same time.

To knit two stitches together insert the right-hand needle through the loops of both stitches from front to back and work a normal knit stitch.

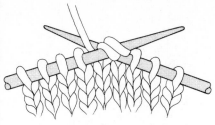

Knitting two stitches together.

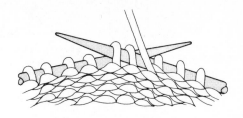

Purling two stitches together.

Similarly if they are to be purled together insert the needle through the loops of both stitches from the back to the front and work a normal purl stitch.

This is abbreviated to 'K2 tog' or 'P2 tog'.

Just as normal stitches can be worked through the back of the loop, so stitches being decreased can be produced by working through the back of both loops at once.

For this the abbreviation is 'K2 tog tbl' or 'P2 tog tbl'.

Sometimes more than two stitches are worked together in this way. The abbreviation will tell you how many.

Stitches can be decreased at any point of the row as required, or they may be worked at the extreme edge. When they are at the edge they are 'lost' in the making up.

By placing them several stitches in from the edge, they can be used to emphasize the seam decoratively after making up.

They may also be used decoratively, further in from the edge, to create the appearance of a seam where no seam exists as in the gores of a skirt.

For both of these reasons it is necessary to know how to decrease so that the stitches lie to the right or left. On a raglan seam the decrease at the right side usually follows the slope of the fabric and the same on the left side.

The 'K2 tog' decrease lies towards the right and is therefore perfect for working at the left side of such a piece of work.

But what about the right-hand side?

To get the decrease to slope towards the left there are three things you may do.

When you have reached the two stitches to be decreased, slip the first stitch, keeping the yarn at the back or behind the stitch. Knit the next stitch and then, with the tip of the left needle, lift the slipped stitch over the knitted stitch.

This is called 'slip 1, knit 1, pass slip stitch over' and is abbreviated to 'Sl 1, K1, psso' or may be 'Sl 1, K1, PSSO'.

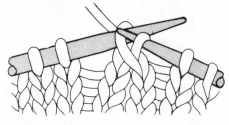

A slip 1, knit 1, pass slipped stitch over decrease, lifting the slipped stitch over.

Always read this carefully in instructions because the number of stitches can vary. It is often used when you slip one stitch, knit the next two stitches together and then pass the slipped stitch over the stitch made by taking two stitches together. In this instance it is called 'Sl 1, K2 tog, psso'.

The second method of making the decrease slope towards the left is to work the two stitches through the back of the loops.

The third method is the least used in this country but makes a much neater pair for 'K2 tog' decreases.

Work the required number of edge stitches to the two stitches to be decreased. Slip each of the next two stitches knitwise and separately from the left to the right needle.

Insert the left-needle tip through the fronts of both stitches together and knit them from this position.

This is one of the things you will have to carry out in creating your own designs, or you will have to remember as I do to substitute for 'Sl 1, K1, psso' whenever you meet it in printed instructions. You will be well rewarded: the result is very much neater.

Because it is unusual, it has no standard abbreviation and in my knitting language has always been exactly as it is 'ssk', but do remember that this is one of the times when the slip purlwise rule is broken and that the two slip stitches must be slipped knitwise. Alter the abbreviation to 'S2, K2 tog' if you think you are likely to forget.

'Paired' decreases are used where stitches need to slope in opposite directions visibly as on a raglan shaping.

Decreasing may often be worked only on the knit side of stocking stitch, but in that case you will know now what to do.

Sometimes, however, decreases may be worked on both sides of the fabric and must also be made to match.

The 'P2 tog' decrease actually slopes to the left when the purl side is the right side of the work. If the purl side is the wrong side of the work then it is worked at the beginning of the purl row.

When the work is turned round to the right side it will then show up as a decrease sloping towards the right.

The decrease used at the end must slope the opposite way and can be made by two methods.

The first way is to 'P2 tog tbl', or purl two stitches together through the back of the loops.

The second is again an unusual decrease worth remembering, and for most knitters is easier to work than the twist required to work 'P2 tog tbl'.

Work to the two stitches to be decreased. Purl the next stitch and slip it back to the left-hand needle.

With the tip of the right-hand needle lift the stitch beyond it over it, and then return the purled stitch to the right-hand needle because it has already been worked.

It is like a 'psso' in reverse, but you must be careful to remember that the first stitch has to be returned to the right hand needle and don't make the mistake of working it again.

This I have always called 'P1 lso', but perhaps you can think of something better.

Design Notes

We are used to seeing decreases beautifully arranged to slope in the same way as the seam they are emphasizing. Why not be different and make the decreases slope the opposite way?

Instead of decreasing one stitch at each end of every right side row on stocking stitch for a raglan, decrease two stitches on every fourth row.

There are fewer methods of decreasing in everyday use than there are methods of increasing. But this need not necessarily be so.

The lace method of making a hole, as we have seen in the 'yon' and 'yrn' increase, can be used along with a decrease.

When you want to decrease one stitch with a lace 'hole' as well, you could try this. Knit to the line of decrease, put the yarn over the needle and knit the next three stitches together. Work a purl row next and then another decrease row and soon the 'yon' stitches will form a lacy ladder.

A little experiment will soon show you many interesting ideas on these lines.

Marker Loops

When increases or decreases are used decoratively as well as to shape the fabric it is often useful to place 'marker loops' so that you can see exactly where they are on the row.

Make a knotted loop in a piece of yarn of a contrasting colour. Before you work the shaping, slip the loop on to the right-hand needle tip after the last stitch you worked.

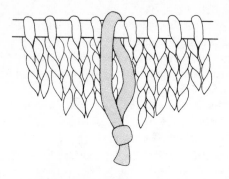

A marker loop positioned in the row, to be slipped as it is reached and carried up row by row as the work continues.

Work the shaping and continue the row. On the next and following rows simply slip the loop from left to right needle, taking care not to knit it into the fabric. In this way it will always mark the position in the row of the last shaping and remind you as well that there are more to follow.

Needle Sizes and Shaping

Increases and decreases can sometimes be made by varying needle size. When a design requires width without shaping, it is sometimes possible to use one size larger needle. After several inches it may be possible again to increase the needle size.

The same can be worked in reverse for decreasing.

Use this technique sparingly!

The initial texture of the stitch or acceptability of the fabric may be entirely altered.

Long lace-patterned skirts, or wide-patterned sleeves may be worked in this way where the design allows the pattern to become less close, without loosing its character and texture.

Mass Shaping

Casting on or off is the best way to add or subtract large numbers of stitches, for instance for kimono sleeves.

The method of casting on and off that you have learned can be used at the beginning of a row, although unless you break the yarn and rejoin it you can not use these methods at the end of a row.

On most designs, if the cast on or off is required at both sides, it is worked at the beginning of the next two rows.

When you are working with very thick needles and yarn it may be necessary to work both ends on the same row so that they are not 'out of line' by the depth of one row.

In this case it is necessary to break the yarn, but on the majority of designs the depth of one row is too small to worry about.

Geometric Shape

Cast on a few stitches. Work in rows where on every second row you increase four times. Keep the increases in line and you will find that you are beginning to get four panels and can finish up with a piece of work with seamed sides forming a flat, square shape.

Increases placed to form a square.

The number of rows worked between the increase rows may depend on the thickness of yarn and needles in order to get a square that will lie flat, but this is simply a matter of tension.

A circle can be worked in a similar way by increasing six or eight times on a row and placing the increases so that they are evenly spaced but not in straight lines.

The same piece of work made with the increases in straight lines will make a six- or eight-sided shape.

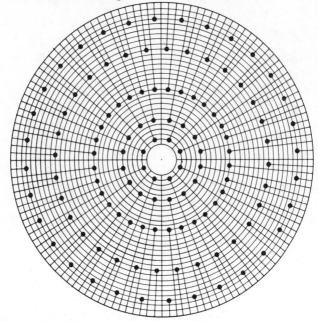

Increases placed to form a circle.

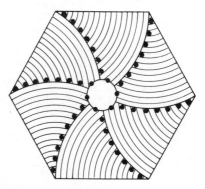

Increases placed to form a six-sided figure.

To lie flat the shaping must be worked with the correct number of rows between.

If you leave fewer rows between the increases, you will find you have created a square which won't lie down, in other words the top part of a pyramid, or a circle that frills like a doiley round the edge or stands up in the middle like a cap or half a toy ball.

Begin to combine them and you are getting shape indeed.

Pieces of work which lie flat can always have an alteration made to the edge where many more increases are worked so that it truly becomes frilled.

5. Creating Solid Patterns

Stitches Forming Vertical Lines

The simple knit and purl stitches are the basis of a great many straightforward designs. They are also used for the family of stitches forming vertical lines.

Many of the patterns in this group are called 'ribbing'.

Not only do they form upright lines on the fabric, but, because of the arrangement of the loops and the smooth side of the stitches, they provide a knitted 'elastic' which also gives a firm edge.

Because it is elastic it also draws the width of a sweater into a hip-fitting 'welt', or it makes warm cuffs that hug the wrist but are still wide enough to take the whole hand.

One and One Ribbing

This is made of vertical lines formed by single knit-and-purl stitches arranged so that lines of smooth stitches are alternated with lines of the looped side of stitches.

Cast on an even number of stitches, like 12 or 16.

1st row Knit one stitch, bring the yarn forward ready to work the next stitch which you need to purl, then take the yarn back so that you can work another knit stitch.

Continue in this way, working one stitch knit and one purl all along the row.

Turn the work so that the needle with the stitches is in your left hand and work another row in the same way.

Work twelve rows.

Always remember to put the yarn into the right position for the next stitch. If you take it over the needle, because you forgot to get it right before starting the stitch, you will make extra stitches.

You can cast off in rib by casting off as you did before but knitting those stitches which the ribbing says should be knitted and purling those that need to be purled.

If you are still using wool and not cotton or man-made fibre you will be able to see how elastic this rib is.

This has taken quite a lot of space to write. All we really needed to say was:

1st row *K1, P1, repeat from * to the end of the row.

The word 'repeat' is usually abbreviated to 'rep'.

Try the next rib to see how even a small difference in design makes a big difference to the fabric.

Two and Two Rib

Cast on an even number of stitches divisible by 4, like 12, 16 or 20.

1st row   *K2, P2, rep from * to end of row.

Repeat the 1st row until you have worked twelve rows or until the rib is deep enough for you to see how it differs from the first rib you made.

Both of these ribs have had an even number of knit and purl stitches. Other combinations are possible.

Three and One Rib

Cast on a number of stitches divisible by 4.

1st row   *K3, P1, rep from * to end of row.

2nd row   *K1, P3, rep from * to end of row.

Repeat the 1st and 2nd rows until the work is long enough for you to see.

This is the first time that the rows have not been the same on both sides.

The wide stripes could have been wider, but you will see that it is not as elastic.

When the wide stripe is made even wider it makes an excellent fabric for sweaters and sports wear, but it needs to be edged with a finer rib – the base of the wide stripes will tend to curl because they are stocking stitch.

Opposite top row: Moss stitch.   Double moss stitch.   Basket stitch.
Opposite middle row: Ridged edging.   Diamond brocade.   One and one rib.
Opposite bottom row: Two and two rib.   Three and one rib.   Wager welt.

Squared Patterns

Only a slight variation to one and one rib gives something quite different.

Moss Stitch

Cast on an odd number of stitches like 15 or 17.

1st row   K1, *P1, K1, rep from * to end of row.

Repeat the 1st row until there are sufficient rows for you to see the stitches clearly.

You will see that the vertical lines have gone completely, but there are still an equal number of knit and purl stitches and they are evenly distributed on both sides of the fabric.

Once again, like garter stitch we have a fabric that will lie flat, but it has lost the elastic quality.

Double Moss Stitch

Cast on a number of stitches divisible by 4, plus 2.

1st row   K2, *P2, K2, rep from * to end of row.

Repeat the first row until you can see the pattern clearly. Larger groups of knit and purl stitches make another variant.

Basket Stitch

Cast on a number of stitches divisible by 6.

1st row   *K3, P3, rep from * to end of row.

2nd row   Work as given for the 1st row.

Repeat the 1st and 2nd rows once.

5th row   *P3, K3, rep from * to end.

6th row   Work as given for the 5th row.

Repeat the 5th and 6th rows once.

Repeat these eight rows twice more, or until you can see the pattern clearly.

Again this pattern will lie flat but it is not elastic.

The pattern could be made in much bigger squares and also a great many variations.

See what happens when you work only three rows before changing.

You will not get a square check, because stitches are not square. They are always wider than they are deep.

Horizontal Patterns

There are times when horizontal lines can be incorporated into a design, particularly on border edges, cuffs, or even on larger areas.

Again the rough and smooth fabrics of stitches are used together.

Wager Welt

Cast on any number of stitches.

Knit seven rows.

Purl one row.

Repeat these eight rows until you can see the pattern.

Although only one row is purled it makes quite a stripe across the rest of the garter-stitch rows.

Ridged Edging

The curl that has been noticed on stocking-stitch fabric because all the loops are on one side can also be used as a design feature.

Cast on any number of stitches.

Beginning with a P row work five rows stocking stitch (that is P1 row, K1 row, P1 row, K1 row, P1 row).

Now repeat the last five rows several times until you get a ridged or concertina effect.

The use of knit and purl stitches together can be made into intricate patterns, as can be seen on some of the east coast fishermen's sweaters of the last century.

These patterns were so distinctive that each small village had its 'own' pattern, by which the crews of its boats could immediately be identified.

Knitted closely, in comparatively fine yarn, the jerseys, or 'ganseys' as they were called, were knitted by the womenfolk for their sons and husbands and provided many years of wear. A new 'gansey' might well be a wedding garment, sometimes with the man's initials or date of birth or marriage knitted into the pattern. Purl stitches formed the letters against a smooth stocking-stitch background.

These garments were usually knitted seamlessly, a method of working which will be described in chapter 9.

Further back in history a patterned silk shirt was worn by Charles I when he was beheaded. A gruesome but a perfect example of pattern produced by placing knit and purl stitches. The borders and main pattern were complicated in arrangement, but the yoke

Patterned shirt worn by Charles I on the day of his death.

was a simple diamond pattern, useful for many types of fabric and fashionable throughout the years.

Diamond Brocade

Cast on a number of stitches divisible by 6 plus 1 extra stitch, for example 25, 37.

1st row   K3, *P1, K5, rep from * to last 4 sts, P1, K3.

2nd row   P2, *K1, P1, K1, P3, rep from * to last 5 sts, K1, P1, K1, P2.

3rd row   *K1, P1, K3, P1, rep from * to last st, K1.

4th row   *K1, P5, rep from * to last st, K1.
5th row   As 3rd row.
6th row   As 2nd row.

Repeat the last six rows until the pattern is long enough for you to see clearly.

This is only a brief look at the patterns that can be made in this way. Many other examples can be found in a stitch dictionary.

6. Creating Simple Lace Patterns

For all those who have not yet added to their needle range this is the moment to do so.

You will certainly need a pair of No 10, 9 and 7 needles. Sizes 11 and 12 are used fairly often, as are 6 and 5, depending on whether you want to knit a reasonable number of thicker garments.

Lace patterns can still be worked in double knitting, but it is advisable to try out 4 ply and 3 ply yarns, or they will feel exceedingly strange when you do eventually come to use them.

Lace patterns can be made using several different techniques. None of these methods is more difficult to work than the ways of creating stitches that you have already practised.

There is nothing in the most complicated pattern that is difficult if you understand what you are doing to the stitches and what you achieve by doing it.

Lace is often made by grouping increasing along with decreasing. The usual increase is the one where the yarn is taken over or round the needle, and the made stitch is worked into on the following row. In this way the pattern is given a 'hole' at the same time as the stitches are drawn sideways in one direction or the other, so emphasizing the pattern.

Lace could be said to be decorative use of 'holes' joined together by the stitches of the fabric!

Miniature Leaf Pattern

Cast on a number of stitches divisible by 6, plus 1 extra stitch, for example 25, 43 stitches.

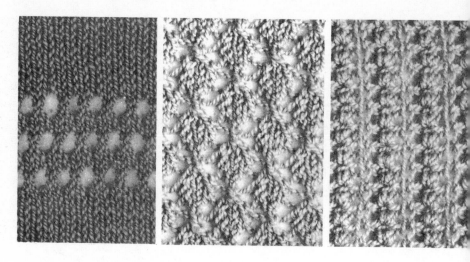

1st row   K1, *K2 tog, yon, K1, yon, ssk, K1, rep from * to end.
2nd row   Purl.
3rd row   K2 tog, *yon, K3, yon, s1 2 knitwise – K1 – p2sso, rep from * to last 3 sts, ssk.
4th row   Purl.
5th row   K1, *yon, ssk, K1, K2 tog, yon, K1, rep from * to end.
6th row   Purl.
7th row   K2, *yon, sl2 knitwise – K1 – p2sso, yon, K3, rep from * to last 2 sts, K2.
8th row   Purl.

Repeat the last eight rows until you have worked as much as you require.

In patterns like this the wrong side row may be purl throughout the lace. It is usual in instructions to find that space is saved by, instead of printing the 4th, 6th and 8th rows, which are all the same the 2nd row printing like this – '*2nd and all even rows* P'.

The word 'even' may be substituted with 'wrongside', 'rightside' or 'alternate' without changing the fact that every other row is purled.

Old Shale

Another lace, much used in the making of Shetland shawls, creates not only a lace pattern, but, by the grouping of several increases and decreases together, a wavy appearance across the fabric. So well known is this lace that it has many different names, including

Rows of eyelet holes.

Miniature leaf stitch.

Indian Pillar stitch, showing the traditional wrong side.

Old Shale stitch.

Picot eyelet diamond pattern.

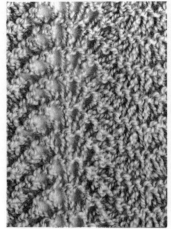

'Feather and Fan'. Old Shale or Shell is believed to be so called after the undulating wave pattern made on sand or shale beaches.

Cast on a number of stitches divisible by 18, for example 36.

1st row K.

2nd row P.

3rd row *(K2 tog) 3 times, (yon, K1) 6 times, (K2 tog) 3 times, rep from * to end of row.

4th row K.

These four rows form the pattern repeat and can be worked until you see the pattern. When you cast off the last row you will also see clearly how the 'wave' effect is formed.

Eyelet Lace Patterns

Lace holes can also be grouped wherever they are wanted; to form straight lines for ribbon slotting, to be arranged as a lace 'flower' or eyelet.

Chain eyelet, usually used to carry ribbon trimming, is made by placing the yarn over the needle followed immediately by the decrease.

Cast on a number of stitches divisible by 2, plus 1 extra stitch.

Knit one row. Purl one row.

Eyelet row K1, *yon, K2 tog, rep from * to end.

4th row Purl.

Repeat these four rows twice to see the effect obtained.

Larger eyelets can be made by working a decrease at either side

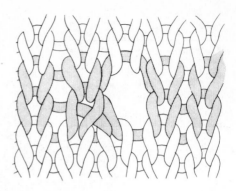

Making an eyelet hole.

of an eyelet made by taking the yarn either once or twice round the needle.

On the following row if the yarn has been taken round the needle once it is still essential to work into it twice, by knitting and then purling into the same loop so that the correct, or starting, number of stitches is retained.

To enhance the decorative effect in the pattern, put the yarn twice round the needle, then work twice into it on the following row. This forms a 'picot' or tiny decorative point in the centre of the eyelet.

Picot Eyelet Diamond

Cast on a number of stitches divisible by 10, plus 2 stitches extra.

1st row　K.

2nd row　P.

3rd row　K2, *K2, K2 tog, y2rn, ssk, K4, rep from * to end.

4th row　P2, *P3, P the 1st loop and K the 2nd loop, P5, rep from * to end.

5th row　K.

6th row　P.

7th row　K2, *(K2 tog, y2rn, ssk) twice, K2, rep from * to end.

8th row　P2, *(P1, P 1st loop and K 2nd loop, P1) twice, P2, repeat from * to end.

Repeat these eight rows as required.

Drawn Stitches in Lace

Lace patterns do not need to have specially made holes. Some patterns become 'lace-like' if the stitches are worked in fine yarn on relatively thick needles and have stitches that are drawn together, leaving lace-like areas at the side of the groups.

Indian Pillar Stitch and Blackberry Stitch, known in some districts as Bramble Stitch, are good examples of this more delicate approach to lacy textures.

Indian Pillar Stitch

Traditionally the row worked in purl is the right side of this pattern, but I have successfully used the 'wrong' side, even when designing a layette for a royal baby, using 1 ply yarn and No 9 or 10 needles.

The finest of all knitting, a 'ring' shawl made in Unst in Shetland.

To get a really lacy effect, you will need to use as fine a yarn as possible, either 2 ply or at the thickest 3 ply, with No 6 or 7 needles.

Cast on a number of stitches divisible by 4, plus 3 extra stitches, for example: 23, 39.

1st row   P.

2nd row   K2, *insert needle through the next 3 sts tog as if to P them but instead work P1–K1–P1 into them so taking 3 sts tog but making 3 sts out of them, K1, rep from * to last st, K1.

These two rows form the pattern and are repeated as required.

Note that after the 2nd row has been worked there should be the same number of stitches on the needle as there were before working it.

The most beautiful lace knitting is probably found in the famous 'ring' shawls made from the finest lambswool in the most northerly of the Shetland Islands. These shawls were named 'ring' because, large though they are, their fineness is such that they can be drawn easily through a wedding ring.

They were copied originally from Spanish lace samples taken to the island by a lady on the 'Grand Tour'.

The shawls were worked so that only one side of the original square was cast on. Even when bordered and lace-edged every possible method was used to avoid the hard lines that would make them more dense.

For lace knitting check that you know how to cast on to avoid a firm line.

Lengthening Stitches

One method of creating a lacy appearance without necessarily using very fine yarn is to lengthen stitches so that more open areas are formed in solid surroundings.

To lengthen a stitch the yarn is wound round the needle tip before drawing it through as the new loop, not once, but twice, or possibly more often, as stated in the instructions.

In the following row the 2nd loop is dropped, which lengthens the remaining loop which is knitted or purled in the ordinary way.

This is usually abbreviated to 'y2rn'. If the number of times is to be more than 2, the number would show how many times was required.

This method can be used very simply on stocking stitch where every 8th row is lengthened, producing a simple alteration in texture and density without creating a very noticeable pattern.

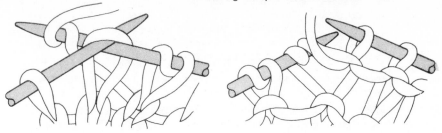

Winding the yarn twice round the needle to lengthen a stitch.

Many more variations of these and other lace patterns can be found in stitch dictionaries.

7. Creating Pattern by Moving Stitch Positions

Moving single stitches or groups of stitches from one position to another brings many design possibilities.

To Add to your Equipment

Add a small cable needle to your equipment before you try this technique. Any not-too-long double-pointed needle will do, but the short, specially made cable needles are easier to use as there is not so much of them.

They can be bought in more than one thickness, but the size is not as important as with knitting needles, provided the stitches you are moving are not forced on to too thick a needle. Cable needles are single short needles designed purely for holding a small number of the stitches for a short time until you are ready to move them round the front or back of the work.

Moving the Position

Until now all the stitches we have been concerned with have been worked immediately above the stitch in the previous row.

Basically there are two ways of moving stitches: twisting and cabling.

Twisting Stitches

To twist or change the position of two stitches side by side it is possible to knit them out of order without the use of a third needle.

To twist two stitches the second is knitted or purled first by passing the tip of the right-hand needle behind or in front of the first stitch. The first stitch is then worked before the left-hand needle is withdrawn from working the other stitch. Once both are worked the left-hand needle can be withdrawn allowing the stitches to take up their new positions.

This is not nearly as complex to work as it sounds in words.

The diagram shows two knit stitches being 'twisted' or crossed so that the right one will lie over the top of the left one.

Knit to the two stitches to be crossed. Pass the tip of the right-hand needle behind the first stitch on the left-hand needle and knit the second stitch, but leave the left-hand needle still in the base of the stitch. Now knit the first stitch that was passed, then slip the left-hand needle out, leaving the two twisted or crossed stitches on the right-hand needle.

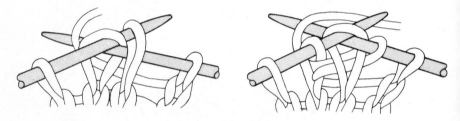

Knitting into the second stitch in twisting stitches.

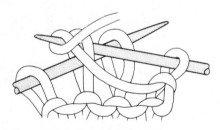

Purling into the second stitch when twisting stitches.

Where twisted stitches are going to form a vertical rib you may often find, as in a wheatear rib, that the cross to the right is worked on every right side row and the cross to the left is worked on every wrong side row.

Wheatear rib stitch.

Wheatear Rib

Cast on a number of stitches divisible by 7, for example: 28, 42.
1st row   P3, *pass tip of right-hand needle behind next st on left-hand needle and K 2nd st then into 1st st, P5, rep from * until 4 sts remain, cross the next 2 sts as before, P2.
2nd row   P3, *pass the tip of the right-hand needle in front of the 1st st on the left-hand needle and P next st then P the 1st, K5, rep from * to last 4 sts cross the next 2 sts as before, K2.
    Continue until the pattern is the required length.

Travelling Stitches

This same method can be used where single stitches travel across a background to make a lattice pattern, either as a panel or an all-

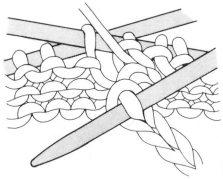

Holding a single stitch in front on
a cable needle when working a
single stitch lattice.

over design. Using a cable needle will give a neat effect when the pattern calls for a single travelling knit stitch on a purl ground.

The stitch that is to be moved is simply slipped on to the cable needle and held at the front of the work until the stitch beyond has been completed, then the stitch on the cable needle can be knitted back on to the right-hand needle.

Cabling Stitches

Fascinating rope-like patterns can be made by altering the position of groups of stitches.

The variety of design comes from the ability to cross to front or back groups from a main or thick rope and, within that rope itself, to divide again so that complex intertwining and plaited effects may be obtained. And, pleasure of pleasures, the most complex rope is no more difficult to work than a simple cross-over, and is easily followed once you have begun the pattern.

Try a simple cable first and then you will be able to see for yourself.

Cast on a number of stitches divisible by 9, plus 3 extra stitches.

1st row   P3, *K6, P3, rep from * to end.
2nd row   K3, *P6, K3, rep from * to end.
3rd row   Work as given for 1st row.
4th row   Work as given for 2nd row.
5th row   P3, *slip the next 3 K sts on to a small cable needle and place at the back of the work, K the next 3 sts from the left-hand

 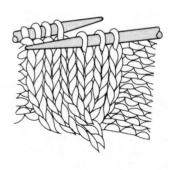

Holding 3 stitches at the back when cabling.
Holding 3 stitches at the front when cabling.

needle and then K the 3 sts from the cable needle, P3, rep from * to end.
6th row   As given for 2nd row.

7th row   As given for 1st row.
8th row   As given for 2nd row.

Repeat these rows at least twice more, until you can see the rope-like twist the K stitches are being given.

In this pattern the left-hand group of stitches crosses in front of the other group and so the rope twists each time from left to right.

If you try the same pattern, but hold the stitches on the cable needle at the front of the work instead of the back, you will alter the direction of the twist to a slope from right to left.

When two ropes or large groups of stitches are placed side by side half can be made to twist in one direction and half in the other, repeating at each cross or separating and coming back together at the following cross.

That, believe it or not, is all there is to cabling.

The first time you work a cable pattern from printed instructions you may find that you have to read every word of the first few rows, turning to abbreviations often, and making very slow progress. But take heart, for the moment a few inches of the pattern have been worked, you can see what you are doing. In fact the pattern is so definite that it becomes difficult to make a mistake.

The Aran sweaters so popular for their chunkiness are often based largely on the combination of travelling stitches, cable and twisted stitches or cables which meet and vere off again forming diamonds.

Abbreviations for cable designs are usually individual to the design. There are so many variations in numbers, rows between cablings and general pattern that they are always fully explained on the pattern for that specific design.

8. Creating Pattern with Colour

Working in Stripes

Striping is one of the simplest ways of adding colour, and as soon as you have mastered stocking stitch and garter stitch you are also capable of working in stripes.

When narrow horizontal stripes are being worked and when the colour you want to start using is already joined to the same side it is easy to carry the yarns up the side of the work. This avoids continually cutting the yarn.

Even if the stripes are fairly wide, there is no need to cut and rejoin the yarn provided it is to be used again at the same side. Twist it in with the yarn in use as you reach the side of the work each time then it can gradually climb the side of the work with the row you are working on. In this way the work will not become puckered or pulled by trying to take it too far in one movement.

Leaving Ends

When ends have to be cut for finishing later never make the mistake of leaving too short an end. It can be very difficult to make a short end secure and if it works loose it may cause dropped stitches.

Joining Colours

To get a straight unbroken line of colour on stocking stitch join the yarn on any row, but this is not the rule if it is reversed stocking stitch.

On garter stitch if you want a straight line the yarn must be joined on right side rows. Joining on wrong side rows will have a looped broken line of colour.

Similarly, if you are working in striped rib you can only obtain an unbroken line of colour if you stop the rib for one row and work, on the right side, one knit row using the new colour, or, on the wrong side, one purl row.

Again the broken line may well be incorporated into the pattern. It simply depends on how you want the finished pattern to look.

Some people feel that the broken line looks wrong and shows a lack of knowledge of how to obtain what might be called the 'right' appearance.

However, in design nothing is wrong if it achieves the effect you intend. It is only wrong when the result does not please you, or produces bad workmanship.

Vertical Stripes

Vertical stripes are worked in a different way.

It is not usual to work many narrow vertical stripes on a garment. This effect is obtained more easily by knitting across the garment instead of up and down.

Vertical stripes usually allow for a ball of the main colour to be used at either side of the stripe or stripes, and separate balls to be used for each stripe.

Worked just in this way an openwork line would tend to appear at the sides of each stripe, but if the strands of yarn are twisted round each other when changing colour the edge of the contrast will remain neat.

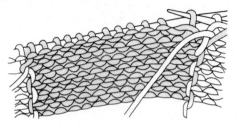

Linking the yarn on the wrong side to avoid gaps when knitting vertical stripes.

When the last stitch of one colour has been worked, lay the colour to the left and bring the next colour to be worked into place round it, so twisting it into place and holding it.

When the stripe is complete the same method is followed. The colour is laid to the left and the other colour picked up catching it in place.

On the following row the yarn will twist in the opposite direction and so a neat ladder of intertwined stitches will be formed on the wrong side at each of the stripe or stripes.

Working Fairisle

'Fairisle knitting' is often inaccurately used to describe any pattern worked in stocking stitch which uses more than one colour. Fairisle really applies only to the very distinctive patterns from the Shetlands.

These designs were allegedly copied from the bright coloured waistcoats found on Spanish sailors washed up during the times of the Armada and are based on X and O shapes with a cross often dominating the design. The designs are based on small motifs, not on the large patterns common to Norwegian knitting.

One other peculiarity of true Fairisle knitting is that only two colours are ever worked in any one row. The design frequently changes its colour to produce a toning effect and the background is also changed, with the same result.

Left: Mock fairisle pattern.

Centre: Rose tweed stitch.

Right: An example of modern fairisle knitting.

Many all-over patterns which use one or more colours are simply this and are more correctly titled 'jacquard' patterns after the Frenchman who first produced a loom to weave these more complicated colour-change fabrics.

There are two different ways of working Fairisle patterns, one is called 'stranding' and the other 'weaving'. In both cases the names refer to the way in which the yarn is carried across the back of the work from one colour group to the next.

Stranding

Stranding occurs when the yarn is carried directly from the last stitch worked in that colour to the next stitch that is to be in that colour. In true Fairisle work the gaps between one colour and the next are seldom large. In using this method it is necessary to watch that you keep the yarn fairly loose across the intervening stitches or the work will be puckered when it is complete. Do not leave slack loops behind, but just enough to cover the stitches between with ease. They are then secured in place by working the next group.

For knitters who work a lot of Fairisle patterns, stranding is much quicker to work as its originators work with one colour round a finger of the right hand and the other colour round a finger of the left hand. The colour required is simply flicked into place. Needless to say, this takes a little practice!

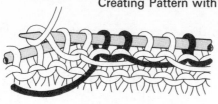

Fairisle stranding.

Weaving

Weaving certainly means a little more work, but it is possible that you may find it easier to achieve correct tension.

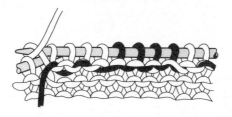

Fairisle weaving.

As soon as one colour is 'out of use' it is twisted with the next colour each time and the other colour works another stitch. In this way it is carried along the row and is in position the next time it is needed when it in turn is twisted with the last colour.

Combining Both Methods

True Fairisle is worked in traditional soft 3 ply yarns. If you are working in heavier yarns it is often better not to twist the yarn on every stitch but to twist it every second or third stitch. This makes a slightly less dense fabric behind the pattern on the wrong side and will lie flat when pressed.

The yarn should certainly never be carried over more than three stitches or again it will tend to leave a loop too easily caught and dragged when the garment is worn.

Working Single Motifs

Sometimes one large motif is placed in a main position on a sweater or several smaller motifs may be placed so that they cannot be classed as an all-over pattern.

In this case it is better to use separate balls of the background colour at each side of the motif so that the yarn does not need to be carried right across the motif on each row.

This is particularly so when the motif is solid as in the case of a square or a large spot. In this case the background colour may not be seen from one side to the other.

The only exception to this is when the background colour peeps through the motif in every other stitch or so. Then there is nothing to gain by using extra balls.

Reading Two-Colour Instructions

When more than one colour is used there are two ways in which the instructions may be written down.

In Words

Where words only are used then letters are usually chosen to represent the different colours used. Sometimes these are chosen alphabetically or sometimes they may be the initial of the colour used. In other words you may have A, B and C which will be marked in the instructions as standing for white, green and red, or you may have W, G and R standing for the same colours.

Whichever form is used it is usually made clear at the start of the instructions.

In Chart

The pattern itself may determine the form used. The previous method can look very complex when a row reads like this:
1st row   K16B, 5W, 3R, 1W, 1B, 1W, 3R, 1W, 2B, 3W, 4R.

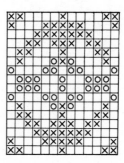

What a fairisle pattern chart may look like.

Then it may be better to make a small map of the pattern on squared paper with a key at the side to indicate which shape on the 'map' indicates which colour.

This method is visual, the knitting can be looked at as it grows, so this is often the quickest method. It lets you see at a glance what you are aiming at and saves you a lot of reading time.

There are however, other ways of producing jacquard-like patterns. In one, a motif is repeated all over the fabric, not unlike Fairisle. In the other smaller patterns two or more colours give interesting textures and knitted tweed-like patterns.

The first way of working could perhaps be called mock Fairisle. It is easy to work and has several built-in advantages.

Mock Fairisle

This is particularly easy for anyone who finds difficulty in keeping the work smooth and unpuckered, because however many colours are in the finished work only one colour is used at a time on any row.

The surface of the fabric can be either smooth as in stocking stitch, or it can be given an interesting texture by working every second or alternate row in knit.

On the first row each stitch to be in the contrast is knitted. All the other stitches are slipped with the yarn behind the work.

On the second row the same stitches are worked in the same colour. All the other stitches are slipped as before but with the yarn on that side of the work, which is the wrong side. Whether the stitches that are not slipped are knitted or purled depends on whether you want a smooth or slightly embossed surface on the finished fabric.

On the third row the original colour is used and all the stitches which were slipped are worked. The stitches worked on the first and second rows are slipped.

On the fourth row the stitches that were worked in the third row are again knitted or purled with the others being slipped.

One of the advantages of this is that every second or wrong side row is very easy to work because you know you only have to knit or purl the same stitches with the same colour as the row before.

This is not the case with all jacquard patterns. When the pattern alters on the wrong side rows it means continually turning the work to see if the stitches are coming in the right place.

Geometric Pattern in Mock Fairisle

Cast on a number of stitches divisible by 5, plus one extra stitch, using main colour, A.

Knit one row.

2nd row (right side)   Using B, *K4, sl 1ybk (ybk is the abbreviation for yarn back or behind the work), rep from * to last st, K1.

3rd row   Using B, P1, *Sl 1yfwd (yfwd is the abbreviation for yarn forward or in front), P4, rep from * to end.

4th row   Using A, K5, *sl 1ybk, K4, rep from * to last st, K1.

5th row   Using A, P5, *sl 1yfwd, P4, rep from * to last st, P1.

6th row   Using B, K1, *sl 1ybk, K4, rep from * to end.

7th row   Using B, *P4, sl 1yfwd, rep from * to last st, P1.

8th row   As given for 4th row.

9th row   As given for 5th row.

These eight rows from 2nd to 9th row form the pattern repeat.

Work sufficient rows to be able to see clearly the formation of the pattern.

Work another swatch in the same way working the stitches on all wrong side rows K instead of P, and see the difference which this makes to the finished appearance and texture of the fabric.

The following pattern is worked in quite a different way and can be knitted using one background colour and one or as many more colours of contrast as are wanted.

Again it is useful to work it once, using only two colours, and again using three or even four colours to see the difference that is obtained in the finished result.

Tweed Patterns

There are many ways of working with more than one colour which obtain tweed-like fabrics. Some have a colour carried across two rows by slipping certain stitches, others can alternate the right and wrong side of slipped stitches so that sometimes the yarn carried across the back of the work is actually carried across the front as part of the pattern.

To draw stitches out of their straight lines another method may also be used, and that is knitting some stitches into the row below the actual stitch on the needle.

One way of increasing is to knit into the row below the stitch and then into the stitch itself (see page 24). In the tweed pattern that follows stitches are not increased but certain stitches are worked into the row below the actual stitch on the needle. Naturally when the left-hand needle is withdrawn from the loop the stitch 'drops' just one row. The loop of thread which is formed is used to create pattern and also removes the hard line of contrast colour.

English Rose Tweed Pattern

Instructions are given for three colours.

Cast on an even number of stitches, using C.
1st row (right side)   Using A, K1, *P1, K1 into row below next st, rep from * to last st, K1.
2nd row   Using A, K.
3rd row   Using B, K1, *K1 into the row below next st, P1, rep from * to last st, K1.
4th row   Using B, K.
5th and 6th rows   Using C, work as for 1st and 2nd rows.
7th and 8th rows   Using A, work as for 3rd and 4th rows.
9th and 10th rows   Using B, work as for 1st and 2nd rows.
11th and 12th rows   Using C, work as for 3rd and 4th rows.

These twelve rows form the pattern and should be repeated until you reach the required length.

9. Working in the Round

Equipment

A set of needles.
At least one circular needle.

When you have some particular garment in mind check with the instructions before you buy.

If you are buying to use for experimental purposes then a short set of No 9 or 8 needles will always be useful as well as giving you practice.

'Flat' and 'Round' Knitting

So far only 'flat' knitting has been dealt with. This is the name given to knitting which is worked backwards and forwards in rows. It applies only to the way in which it has been knitted and not to the finished shape.

You may have made a ball which was completely round when it was finished but if it was worked in one piece or in sections that were knitted in rows, then it was knitted 'flat'.

What 'in the Round' Means

Knitting or working 'in the round' means that the work is tubular and the knitting proceeds round and round, instead of backwards and forwards.

There are two ways of working in the round.
1. Using sets of needles.
2. Using circular needles.

Using Sets of Needles

Sets of needles consist of four double-pointed needles all of the same size. Needles are sized in the same numbers as pairs of needles, although they do not include the thickest sizes.

In other countries sets may differ by having five needles to a set instead of four.

Because the needles are double-pointed it is possible to go along one needle until all the stitches have been worked then continue along the next needle using the needle which has become spare.

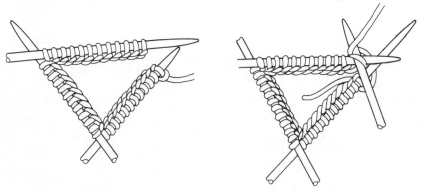

Casting on with three needles, for knitting 'in the round'.

Casting on for Round Knitting.   The methods of casting on remain the same and you can cast all the stitches on to one needle and divide them out to the other two later, or you can cast on one group on one needle, the second group on the next needle, and the third group on the third needle.

When the second method is used, do watch that you keep the yarn taut between the needles or the cast on edge will not be smooth.

To Start Knitting.   Use the spare needle that so far holds no stitches. Draw the last stitch round until it is close to the first stitch.

Insert the spare needle into the first stitch and work in the ordinary way along the first needle.

Continue using the spare needle to work the stitches off the next needle and so on as required.

It is a good idea to place a marker thread at the start of the second round so that you automatically note when you begin a new round. This is particularly necessary where the stitches are evenly grouped and there is no way of recognizing one needle from another.

The Effect on Patterns.   When you first learned to knit you studied carefully the way in which the plain and loop sides of the stitches affected the pattern. Now, although the stitches are the same, there is one great difference in not turning the work.

Knit every row and what do you get? Stocking stitch, because by not turning the work the loops are all on the same side.

Knit one round and purl the other alternately and you will find that now you have garter stitch.

Once again it sounds far more complicated than it is. Once you have tried it and seen it in practice for yourself it will be quite automatic.

Tubular Knitting.   Knitting 'round' produces tubes instead of flat pieces of knitting but there is no need for these to be shapeless. Gloves, mittens and socks are all more shapely and comfortable to wear when they are knitted round than when they have to be worked in rows and seamed.

Circular Needles

Nothing could be worse than 'circular needle' to describe this exceedingly versatile piece of equipment. It is so badly named and so misleading to people who have not actually used them that one manufacturer calls them 'Twinpins' instead. Needle for 'continuous' knitting is perhaps a more accurate description although it may not sound very exciting.

They consist of two pointed needle ends which are securely joined, usually by a slim nylon flex.

They are used for knitting round exactly as a set of needles would be, except that you never reach a point when the needle is free of stitches because they are continually moving round as you work.

This makes it even more necessary to put a marker loop at the

Knitting with circular needles.

start of the second round to show where the round begins. Circular needles have many advantages.

If ever there is a time when you suffer from tired shoulders and arms then you will be particularly glad of these needles.

The weight of the knitting is always moving evenly round the needle so you are not constantly getting all the weight in one hand and then all the weight in the other as happens when you are knitting with pairs of needles.

Fairisle, Norwegian, and in fact any two or more coloured work, becomes additionally easy to work because the right side of the work is always facing you and you can see where you are at a glance instead of having to turn the work over.

Circular needles can obviously be used to cut down the number of seams in skirts and sweaters that are knitted round.

They have, however, a second use which makes them very valuable indeed.

Not only can you knit round with them but they are also just as useful as a pair of needles for knitting rows backwards and forwards.

All that differs is that after casting on, instead of curling them round into a circle and joining the work, you turn the needle and work back the way you have come using the other tip as the second needle.

Perhaps it sounds a little like something out of science fiction but the best thing you can do is to try it out!

Cardigans can be knitted across the full width of back and both fronts up to the armhole, divided, and then each section knitted on up to the shoulder.

Depending on design, the sleeves can probably be picked up around the armhole using a set of needles, and knitted downwards towards the wrist. When there is a button-strip right round the neck the circular needle will be able to hold all the stitches without having to have an unsightly join.

Sweaters, of course, can combine the two techniques, using the needle to knit the body circularly and then using it as a pair of needles to knit back and front up to the neck.

A raglan sweater worked in reverse (starting at the neck and working circularly down to the armholes) can then have the stitches for sleeves left on holders until the main part of the body has been worked. The sleeves can then be completed using a set of needles and you will cast off the last edge with no more sewing up at all.

Joining in New Balls.   In joining in a new ball the end of the new and the end of the old should both be left on the wrong side to darn in later. Take care to leave the end towards the side so that there is no possibility of it spoiling the centre front or back.

The Only Drawback.   Circular needles have just one drawback. You can only knit larger articles with them. There must be enough stitches on the needle to reach from point to point. Therefore bootees and baby garments, gloves, mittens and socks all need to be made using sets of needles.

Circular needles are available in several different lengths. The length you will require will depend on the fewest stitches you are going to work. Although it will only take down to a certain number it will take considerably more than this before it becomes too full.

A table of the number of stitches that the different lengths are capable of handling in different yarn thicknesses is usually included in the pack, and could be checked with the shop assistant if you are uncertain.

An example of this will show exactly what is meant. A No 8 circular needle 16 inches long would need approximately eighty stitches in a good double knitting wool to reach from point to point easily. During working, these stitches could be increased until there were four times as many, about 320, before there were too many for comfortable knitting and before you would need to use a 24 inch needle.

10. Tension and Yarns

To design garments for yourself it is essential that you understand what tension is. It is no less important if you are going to knit successfully garments that other designers have prepared for you.

Tension

Tension is a measurement. It is the number of stitches and rows obtained by the designer over a given area, usually 1 inch, sometimes 2 or 4 inches and more often nowadays over 10 centimetres.

Why Tension is Mentioned

You are going to make a garment that has been designed for you.

It has been designed at the tension that is mentioned. Unless you work at the same tension you can hardly expect to make a similar garment. At a different tension, or a different number of stitches or rows to an inch, the finished measurements will not be the same as the designer obtained.

Tension in knitting is like a signature in writing: it is a personal and individual matter.

This is very important because your tension will be the right and natural way for you to do it and you must not try to alter it however often a friend may tell you that your knitting is too tight or too slack!

You may be a very precise person who likes everything neat, tidy and planned well in advance. You may be a very happy-go-lucky sort of person who takes life as it comes and never worries very much about anything. Much more likely is the fact that you are probably a complex mixture of both. One thing is certain, you will not be an exact copy of your next-door neighbour or even of Mrs So-and-So across the street.

So your knitting tension is unlikely to be exactly the same either. And it is also unlikely to be exactly the same as the designer who originally worked out and wrote the instructions you are going to follow.

Also – How to measure tension correctly
with a pinned out sample swatch.

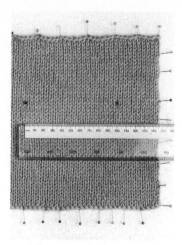

How to Measure Tension

The larger the swatch or sample you make for measuring, the better. Although the number of stitches may be given as over 1 inch or 4 centimetres, you can't be certain of the number of stitches unless your swatch is larger than 4 centimetres or 10 centimetres.

Measure over 4 inches or 10 centimeters and divide the number of stitches by four to see how many stitches there really are in 1 inch or 2·5 centimetres.

In this way you will know more readily if there are four and a half stitches, or even four and a quarter. Measured over a small area, like an inch, or 2·5 centimetres it is very difficult to tell whether there are four stitches or nearly five stitches.

In one inch it may not be important. In the finished garment it is important. Half a stitch might make a difference of several sizes.

Place a pin in the point where the measurement is to start and a pin at the end of the measurement and always use a ruler to measure with the fabric lying on a flat surface.

How to Obtain the Correct Tension

If you find there are fewer stitches to the measurement than there should be then it means that your stitches are larger than those used by the designer, and you should try again using one size smaller needle than is stated.

If you find that there are more stitches than the instructions state, it means that your stitches are too small. You need to try another swatch, using one size larger needle than is stated in the instructions.

The size printed in the instructions is only a guide, and more knitters would meet with immediate success if this were omitted and left blank, to be filled in by the knitter after a trial swatch.

Sometimes, particularly with man-made fibres, it is difficult to obtain both stitches and rows correctly.

In this case the stitches are the most important number to obtain correctly. You will be able to measure the various parts of the garment as you work to check that you are obtaining the correct or required length.

Tension over Irregular Patterns

There are times when the instructions give a tension measured over stocking stitch although you can clearly tell that the actual garment is worked in a chunky, puckered or other distinctive pattern. This is usually the case if a pattern is difficult to lay completely flat.

However, if you work a stocking stitch swatch in your normal knitting, adjusting the needles as necessary, then the same adjustment will be required when you knit the pattern. If you have had to use one size larger to get the right number of stitches over stocking stitch, then you will need to use one size larger when you knit the garment.

Reminder for All

The space in this book is important. The first part of this chapter would not have been included if it had not been of vital importance to your success.

It is much quicker to cast on thirty or forty stitches and work a few inches to check the tension than to knit the whole garment and find it is just too small, or that you have run out of yarn before it is finished. Then you have to pull it all down and start over again or abandon it, wasting money and effort. Check first, and make the garment as you want it right from the beginning.

Tension and your own Designs

When you start to make up your own designs you will quickly learn that an idea will stay just a vague thought until you have tried the stitch you are thinking of using and decide just how it is to look and know what tension you are going to use.

Then, and only then, can you get down to the actual details.

Types of Yarn

In chapter 2 yarns were divided simply into different categories. Before you start to make any garment it is a good idea to check whether you know what you are using or not.

Some yarns are suitable for certain purposes, some for others. It may determine what you are going to use if you know whether it will wash well or whether you may have to have the garment dry-cleaned.

Some yarns tend to stretch when pressed with a hot iron. The spinner of the yarn is the person most concerned that you are satisfied with it and if there is any point, like pressing, which you simply must not do with this yarn, you will find that the ball band will carry a warning about it.

Always check, both from ball and from printed instructions before you start to knit whether there are any such notes. It is easier to do this than by trial resulting in error!

Wools

Wool is available from the finest of lace plys to the chunkiest of quick-to-knit varieties and has few drawbacks unless you consider the fact that it has a tendency to shrink when washed in excessively hot water. The advantages, on the other hand, are elasticity, warmth, durability and no need to avoid pressing.

A smoothly spun wool, like the average 3 and 4 ply and double knitting yarns, also gives a smooth surface when worked in stocking stitch.

Unsmooth Yarns

Nubbly yarns, like bouclé, which come and go according to fashion, are a little more difficult to knit until you have had some experience of knitting, because the yarn does not slip over the fingers so easily and the formation of the stitches is less easy to see. However, they are worth experiment, as many attractive tweed-like fabrics and unusual patterns can be produced by using a plain yarn with a nubbly one.

Using More than One Yarn

Mixing one or more yarns may produce unusual patterns but do mix yarns from similar categories only.

Bouclé wool may very successfully be teamed with a smooth double knitting or 4 ply wool but never mix it with a man-made fibre double knitting.

Mixture Yarns

A slightly different mixing of yarns occurs in those ready mixed for you.

Today many yarns are the best qualities of two threads brought together and spun in this way for you. In this way you may find that wool and nylon are mixed, or two different man-made fibres have been incorporated into the finished product.

Fluffy Yarns

Angora and mohair also tend to be produced according to fashion and are either readily available or not to be found anywhere.

Both make up into garments that are an asset to any wardrobe, but neither is suitable for a beginner's first garment. Try something else first and return to the fluffies when you have had experience.

Metallic Yarns

Do check on washability. Some metallic yarns have to be dry-cleaned.

Most metallic yarns look better if the finished surface is patterned. The patterning can be slight since a complicated pattern is lost in the glitter, but a smooth stocking stitch appears very flat and uninteresting and may be lined or almost striped, depending on the method of producing the yarn.

Man-made Yarns

Particularly with man-made fibres check to see that pressing is advised.

Many of these yarns will produce a non-elastic ribbing, but on the other hand patterns stand out strongly.

The smoothness of the plain side of stocking stitch is often less easy to obtain and you may find that one size of needle used for a knit row is best with a size smaller or larger for the purl row. If the same size is used for both, the resulting fabric may be ridged and uneven.

Because of this tendency to get an uneven surface, continental or twisted stocking stitch is often used most successfully for designs in these yarns.

Cotton, Linen and Silk Yarns

Cotton is an exceedingly useful yarn especially for warm-weather wear. Patterns show up well and stocking stitch is smooth. Pressing is seldom any problem but a certain degree of elasticity is lost from ribbed areas.

Linen and silk tend to be available only when at the height of fashion and are usually both expensive yarns although they make up into beautiful fabrics.

Both have similar characteristics to cotton, and when in fashion should certainly not be overlooked.

Aran Yarns

The real yarn from Aran is creamy coloured and can usually be obtained in a near natural state with some of its lanolin still in the wool. This makes it very suitable for sportswear as to some extent it is rain repellent. Much of this type of yarn is covered by the words 'Aran-type' yarn, as it may easily be man-made as opposed to 100 per cent wool and its production in many colours is due to fashion demand rather than to its original state.

Dye Lots

When a spinner chooses to stock a particular colour the dye is always made up to the same 'recipe'. But after the initial dyeing there may be a slight variance in the finished colour. Wool in the pre-dyed state is seldom the same colour twice which naturally affects the finished result. The colour of the wool before dyeing is affected by the temperature and rainfall of the season, and the amount of grass the grazing sheep have eaten.

None of these need affect you provided you remember to buy enough yarn to complete the garment you are going to make. It is also a good idea to check that the shop assistant gives you balls that all carry the same dye lot number.

When you buy yarn that is of a different make to the yarn specified in the design you are going to make beware of the fact that it may require a different quantity of yarn. Even a small alteration made to the pattern will mean that a different quantity of yarn will be needed to complete the garment.

When you are not quite certain about the quantity, it is a good idea to buy from a shop that will put part of the quantity aside for you for a few weeks. If you do this – do not expect the shop to keep it forever. Your yarn will be taking up space required for new stock, so knit part of the garment and estimate from this just how much more you will need.

Extra yarn is always useful for trying out stitch ideas, or for making small gifts and bazaar items.

11. Reading Instructions

Much thought and experiment has gone into the writing of magazine and leaflet instructions as presented to us today.

The art of writing is to be able to state exactly what the knitter should do. This should not be done in such a way that there is any doubt: there must be only one meaning to the phrase used by the designer.

Already you will have appreciated the need for a 'knitting language' where space is saved by the extensive use of abbreviation.

Correctly, abbreviations should be followed by a full stop or point. This means that sl.1, K.1, p.s.s.o., would look like this. For ease of reading quickly and clearly the full points are usually omitted now and in that case you get sl 1, K1, psso, which you will agree means less to look at.

When you are using a pattern that still has the full point take extra care to see what you read and to read exactly what actually is printed.

Nearly all printed instructions are carefully checked. Spinners' leaflets are very carefully produced and most magazines specializing in knitting patterns have a department whose special task it is to write instructions in the 'format' or 'style' that their particular readers are used to. It is also their task to see that the instructions are correct and that they are checked mathematically.

Occasionally you may find an error because once the checker has misread a phrase she will continue to do so and it will only come to light if someone else notices it. Every effort is made to avoid such errors even to accounting for each stitch on graph paper as an additional physical check against mind-wandering.

It is a wise knitter who, coming across something that reads doubtfully, goes back very carefully over the words, considering why every comma or bracket is there and what they mean before writing off to the source of the pattern, condemning all pattern writers. Once something has been misread by the knitter it is very difficult to see how the designer could easily mean something else.

Paper is expensive and space is important. Anything that is printed in a magazine or on a leaflet is there because the editor considered it was too important to omit, so reading it carefully could make all the difference between success and failure.

Buying a Leaflet

When you buy a pattern, particularly in a departmental store, do be guided by your own judgement rather than that of a shop assistant who may well not even be able to knit!

When the pattern states that it is intended for a certain 3 ply that is what you must get. Four ply in the shade you want (which is not stocked in 3 ply) will not knit to the correct tension, unless the assistant can also sell you a magic wand.

Select the design you want and then buy the yarn that is specified.

If the yarn you need is really unobtainable then consider the leaflets that are available for that yarn.

Still no success? Then return to the first design you chose and see if you know what might be a substitute yarn. Buy only one ball until you have tried to see if you can obtain the correct tension. If you can then certainly it will be safe to make the substitution, provided you remember that this may make a difference to the quantity needed.

The yarn that has been substituted may weigh less or more than the original yarn or may be made up in balls of different yardage.

Measurements

Check that the measurements correspond fairly nearly to those of the person for whom the garment is intended. Simple alterations, particularly in length are not usually difficult to carry out unless

there is a very large motif in several colours used in the pattern.
Any adjustment will alter the number of balls you will need.

Tension

Do read chapter 10.

Also remember that anything written on the instructions is there
because it is considered to be too important to omit.

Before Beginning to Knit

Check tension and materials as well as size and then read through
the list of abbreviations to make certain that you understand them
all.

The majority of abbreviations are common to most instructions,
but if the stitch is unusual the designer may have had to make up
her own.

Cable and Aran patterns may very easily have a pattern you have
worked before but may have a different abbreviation from the one
you are accustomed to. It is much easier to read these beforehand,
although you will no doubt have to refer to them again, than to
try and work out what they mean when you are coping with full
needles and stitches precariously balanced on a cable needle as well.

Also read once through the actual instructions so that you know
how many pieces of knitting you are about to make.

Sometimes garments can be knitted from the neck downwards,
or from side to side. There will always be good reasons for this,
but it can be most disconcerting to be increasing when you think
you should be decreasing, or working side shaping when you have
newly cast on. By reading the instructions first you can be fore-
warned, so saving precious working time . . . and confusion!

Use of the Asterisk *

An asterisk is usually a sign that you repeat from that point.

So far in this book it has been used to mark the start of a group
of words that you have to repeat until you have worked to the end
of a row.

One or two or even more asterisks are sometimes placed before a
row or section to denote that at some point later the instructions
will ask you to return to this point again.

Round Brackets ( )

Brackets are usually placed before and after different sizes or the different number of stitches to be worked for the different sizes given in these instructions.

So where there are four sizes, the number of stitches to be knitted for the first size would come before the bracket, the number of stitches for the second size would come inside the bracket, the third number would come next and the number for the largest size would come last just before the bracket was closed and would look like this.

K2(4:6:8) sts . . .

The numbers inside the brackets are usually separated by a semi-colon ; a colon : or a comma , as is the style of that particular spinner or magazine.

Use of Square Brackets [ ]

Instructions sometimes call for a repeat within a repeat, usually indicated by brackets within asterisks.

Such a row might read – K1, *K1, P4 [K1, K2 tog] 3 times, K1, repeat from * to end.

In such a case not only would you repeat from the * but you would K2 tog 3 times in each repeat as well.

Where different sizes were also involved it might read – K1, *K1, P4 [K1, K2 tog]3 (4:5:6) times, K1, rep from * to end.

Should you find it difficult sometimes to see the difference between : and ; or between , and . try adding a magnifying glass to the contents of your workbag. Some prints can be very difficult to see in certain lights.

How to Measure

Lay the work on a flat surface and measure with a ruler.

Please note – your own lap and quite possibly the arm of your chair are NOT flat surfaces. A table is a flat surface, as long as it is not covered with books or wool.

Completion

The pressing, making-up and even washing instructions are usually exceedingly short but are still included for reading, not just to fill up space.

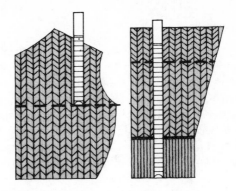

Measuring knitting.

When you are experienced it may be that you can draw on your own knowledge and, by using carefully planned making-up surpass the printed instructions many times over. On the other hand, in this paragraph there is sometimes vital information about pressing, iron heat, or washing which you may not know.

Better to read it and be safe.

12. Finishing your Work

Knitting is what this book is all about, but to show beautiful knitting to its best advantage you must know how to press it, how best to treat and care for it and how to make up your garments so that if anything, you improve your knitting not spoil it.

Bad knitting can never look good just because the making-up is perfect, but good knitting can look really dreadful if the making-up and the seaming of the pieces is poor and badly carried out.

Pressing

Once all the pieces of knitting are finished they will need to be pressed, provided they require it.

Provided they require it does not really mean 'if you think you can skip it or not'. It depends which type of yarn you have used and which stitch patterns are used throughout the garment, including different stitches used for edgings.

When not to Press

The ball or the instructions may state quite clearly that the type of yarn should not be pressed. In such cases DO NOT PRESS IT. Where you have substituted a different yarn for the one specified make certain that you know whether or not it should be pressed.

Certain stitches such as ribbing and garter stitch should not be pressed: they should retain their natural elasticity.

What Pressing Means

Like several other terms in knitting it is a pity 'pressing' is the word used. It implies that pressure on the iron is needed and desirable, which is not really the case.

Most pressing is carried out by placing a damp cloth over the wrong side of the knitting and placing a hot iron on the cloth. The one thing you must avoid is pushing the iron around as if you were ironing. The iron should only be laid lightly on the surface so that the heat of the iron makes the dampness of the cloth into steam which is trapped and forced around the stitches, making them more even than before.

Preparation for Pressing

Once the pieces of a garment are knitted they must be prepared for pressing. If they are pressed just as they happen to be on the ironing table the seams will be irregular and the stitches may not be neatly one above the other since some patterns tend to pull the stitches a little to one side. A badly pressed garment will hang badly.

The preparation for pressing is called 'pinning out'.

Pinning Out. Whatever you are going to press, even a tension square, will tend to curl, so it requires pinning to hold it in position.

Lay the piece of knitting down on your ironing pad (see page 9) with the wrong side facing you and the right side on the pad.

First pin the corners by sticking the pin directly, at a slight angle, through the knitting and into the pad. Make certain that all the stitches are above each other in straight lines and that all the rows across are in straight lines. Then place pins all round the edges preferably $\frac{1}{2}$ inch apart, certainly not more than 1 inch apart.

When you are pinning a piece of knitting make certain that the stitches and rows are even, that it is the width the instructions say

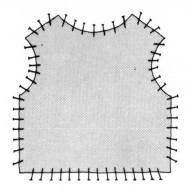

Pinning out knitting ready for pressing.

it should be, and that any curves like armholes are smooth curves.

Putting pins around the edge will not help if the knitting is dragged out to each pin and sinks away again before the next. The smoother the edges and lines, the easier the seaming will be. Pinning is a most tedious job and one that too many people overlook. It is the one job that professionals never ignore. They know only too well that a perfectly pinned garment will be easy to cope with from then on.

How to Press

Once you are certain that the pinning is correct for size and good edges have been achieved, then wet a cloth in warm water and lay it over the knitting.

Hold the iron gently over each section of the knitting in turn until the cloth is dry. This does not mean lean heavily on the iron squashing the poor stitches through the ironing board. This will only flatten the surface of the stitches and, particularly if you have taken all the trouble to knit in a pattern, you will make the pattern less noticeable.

Also lift the iron from one section to the next. If you push it about as you do when ironing you will spoil and distort the lines of stitches.

Remove the cloth once it is dry. If the piece of fabric is properly dry remove the pins.

When two similar pieces of garment such as the two fronts of a cardigan have to be pressed try and press them at the same time and it will be easy to see that you have them both exactly the same size.

Making-up

Using the correct seam and working methodically are the most important points to remember when completing garments.

Instructions do not always give very detailed help and it is best to know the methods so that you can set your own standard and finish with a really perfect garment.

Seaming

The type of edge will determine the seam you use. When you are joining vertical seams that run up and down the garment in the same way as the stitches, then either use backstitch or, preferably the 'invisible' seam.

Backstitch Seam.   When the seam is across the fabric or stitches as a shoulder seam then it is necessary to use a backstitch seam. Seams should always be worked with a blunt-pointed wool needle so that the stitches are not easily split.

A backstitch in knitting is worked the same way as back stitching in sewing except that to get it perfect it is necessay to check continually that you are following a line between stitches rather than through stitches on the side away from you as well as on the side facing.

When the garment is thick it is advisable to use a thinner yarn of the same type and same colour. Sometimes it is possible to untwist the yarn you used for knitting the garment and use fewer threads for sewing.

Seams should never be so slack that you can pull the edges apart and see the stitches nor should they be so tight that they pucker the knitting up forming a hard harsh line.

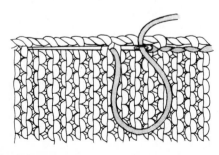

Working a back stitch seam.

Patterns that leave an uneven edge also need backstitched seams.

Remember that the appearance of the seam needs to be good when finished. An oversewn seam will seldom give you a neat straight line so leave it to others.

Invisible Seam.   An invisible seam can be used wherever the two edges to be joined are straight. This applies particularly when the garment is in stocking stitch. The result is a beautiful join, drawing a line of stitches from each side together so that the knitting looks as if it were carried right across, and no seam existed. It is not mentioned in many books in this country and in at least two it is wrongly explained. However, it is very easy to work and worth trying.

It is worked on the right side and it makes no difference whether you work from the top downwards or the bottom upwards.

Secure the end of the yarn you are using at the beginning of the seam and pass the needle under the two strands of yarn between the first and second stitches and draw the yarn through to the right side. Repeat this on the opposite piece to be seamed passing the needle in and under the threads between the top two stitches one in from the edge.

Return to the first side and pass the needle in and under the next two threads and repeat this on the other side.

Work down or up the seam in this way drawing the two edges together as you work.

To use this seam I always work increases or decreases inside one

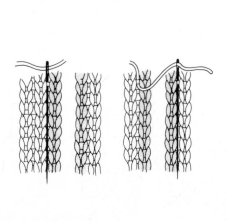

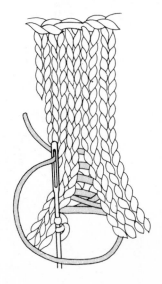

Working an invisible seam.

or two edge stitches so that a perfect join is made between the two edges.

The diagrams show clearly how to work.

Ideally and in very thick yarn it is better to lift only one thread on each side at a time, but on thicknesses up to and including double knitting I find it is quite possible to halve the work by working under two threads at a time.

The stitches must be tight enough to resist pulling apart but must not pucker the work by drawing it tighter than the actual knitting.

Flat Seam. Sometimes it is necessary to have a flat seam, for instance where a button strip joins the main fabric. In this case it is better to work on the wrong side picking up one stitch from one side and moving directly across to one on the other side then one on the first side until a woven seam has been worked.

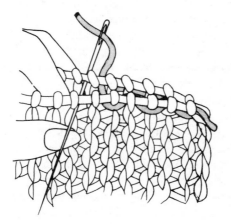

A flat seam.

Forming a Hem

A hem is one method of finishing off an edge without working rows of ribbing, moss stitch or another 'balanced', non-curling stitch. The rows that are intended to be turned on to the wrong side are usually worked a very little tighter than the right side of the work so that they lie neatly in place. When they are worked at the same tension as the right side they tend to push the hem forward, making it more obvious as well as more bulky.

The hem instructions may be given in two ways. You may be told in the instructions to turn so many rows or 1 inch or other

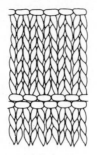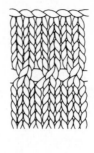

A foldline for a hem, and an eyelet row as foldline.

measurement to the wrong side, or the number of rows that are to form the hem may be marked by a 'fold' row being knitted into the work. On stocking stitch this fold row would consist of one purl row being worked so that it was on the smooth side. The hem would then fold naturally along this line because there would be no loops to take up space along the folding line.

This one row is often also worked using a tighter tension or may be worked into the back of the stitches so that when folded it will sit neatly and closely and not tend to splay out. It may be called a 'fold' row or a 'marker' row.

When pinning a hem in place always fold it directly up on the knitting beyond so that the stitches stay in straight lines and don't get out of line or twist. If they do twist the hem will not lie smoothly but will tend to buckle. When pinning a long hem pin the outer edges or seams first with the stitches directly in line. Then pin it halfway along its length and gradually divide the areas until the pins are close enough together for easy sewing.

Slip stitches very like ordinary hemming can be used, lifting first

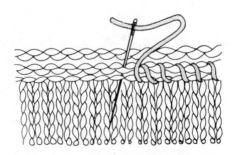

Sewing up a hem.

a stitch from the edge and then just enough of a stitch on the wrong side of the knitting to hold the thread in place. In this way the stitches will not show on the right side, and the hem will remain invisible on the outside of the garment provided you do not pull the stitches too tight. They require to be tight enough to hold the hem just as it was pinned but must not drag against the knitted stitches.

Picking up Stitches

It is often the case that once the garment reaches the making-up stage a neckband or armbands are knitted on and for this stitches have to be 'picked up'. They could be cast on and the band sewn on but this all makes for extra sewing, whereas it is quite easy to knit them directly on to the main section.

This is usually carried out by using a smaller size needle than was used for the main garment and is begun with the right side of the work facing.

Picking up stitches.

Insert the tip of the right-hand needle into the actual fabric one stitch in from the edge, place the end of yarn round the needle and draw one stitch through as if you were working a knit stitch. Other stitches are worked around the edge in the same way until the required number are on the needle. If you experience any difficulty you can use a needle one size smaller, but remember to adjust so that you have the correct tension for the edge to be worked.

Making-up Simplified

The answer to many difficulties both in seaming and in picking up stitches is that you feel you are nearly finished and you just do not take the one particular piece of care that would save a great deal of disappointment. Countless knitters start to sew a button strip on or to pick up 100 stitches along an edge without giving themselves a guiding line to work to.

Before you begin, fold the edge in half and place a pin in as a marker. Fold this in half and place another pin and so on until you have divided the edge into four or eight or whatever seems reasonable for its length. Now do the same with the strip that has to be sewn on. It will then be simple to match pin to pin.

The same applies if you are picking up stitches. It is easy to pick up ten stitches between two pins before you go on and pick up another ten in the next section. You will then have all the stitches you require evenly spaced along the edge.

Avoiding Seams

There are some people who really find it difficult to make up neatly, try as they will, although they may be skilled knitters.

For them it is certainly better to try to avoid as much making-up as possible.

Read the pattern before you begin. Also read chapter 9 because it may be that you can use a Twinpin or circular needle to knit back and fronts together.

Grafting Shoulders

When it comes to shoulder seams the neatest way is to leave each group of stitches on a needle instead of casting them off and then to place front and back edges together and graft the two edges.

Given a little pre-planning you will find there are many ways in which you can avoid the number of seams in the average garment.

Buttons and Buttonholes

Buttonholes and buttons are better strengthened. They will wear better and will not then drag at the knitted fabric you have been at such pains to produce.

Buttonholes

With the exception of eyelet holes on small garments for babies, the average buttonhole requires a row of blanket stitch or buttonhole stitch worked around the edge. There is no need to work a 'bartack' at the ends of the buttonhole as you do on material.

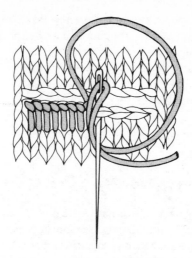

Buttonhole finish.

Use fine yarn of the same type and colour or use a silk or button-hole twist of the same yarn. If the match is difficult, consider using a contrast colour in buttons and thread.

One Tip Worth Knowing.   One tip that is seldom printed concerns buttonholes. Worked as you are usually instructed, by casting off so many stitches on one row and then casting on so many stitches in the following row, you will find a nasty loop of yarn across one corner of the hole. There is absolutely no need for this if you re-member to make this alteration.

On the first row do exactly as instructed and cast off the given number. When you get to the first gap on the next row, instead of casting on the same number as you cast off, work twice into the last stitch before the gap (just like an increase) and then cast on one stitch less than you were told to do.

In actual fact you will have replaced the correct number of stitches, but in a slightly different way. The stitch at the start of the buttonhole where you make the increase, 'takes up the slack' and gives a neat finish instead.

This can be used on buttonholes of any number provided stitches are cast off and then on again.

Buttons

Buttons too are so often left to hang on to the knitting. Even on a baby's jacket they are better for being strengthened. One way of doing this is to sew a tiny scrap of the actual knitting behind. Another is to sew the button on through a line or patch of ribbon so that it takes the strain instead of the knitting.

If you can crochet, a chain worked the required length and caught into place by each button as it is sewn on works admirably.

Take time, making-up does need it.

13. Designing for Yourself

Designing for yourself must be the ideal of all knitters who become good at the craft and who understand how patterns are built up. Once you design your own garments there are no longer any limits to what you can make. The size can be exactly as you want it and the colour and type of yarn can be the ones that you really want.

What Designing Means

Designing and all it implies may be hard to define but it is very easy to say what it is NOT.

You are NOT designing if you use someone else's instructions, find another stitch pattern, or even two, that knit to the same tension and use those instead of the original. Even if you then alter the length you are only adapting.

Designing means starting from the idea, then working out which is the best yarn, colour, stitch pattern or patterns, tension, size, length and buttonholes.

It sounds complex but like many things a start can be made at a simple but satisfying level, for instance, a simple sweater.

The Beginning

The beginning can be made anywhere – it consists of an idea for the sort of sweater you really want. Perhaps you can see it quite clearly in your mind. You may think of it while peeling the potatoes or on top of a bus going to work.

Make a quick sketch of it as soon as possible. Nothing grand, just enough lines to remind you whether it starts with a ribbed edge, is patterned or plain, what sort of sleeves it is going to have and whether the neck is high, wide, shallow or V-shaped.

Buy only one ball of yarn to start with. You will need to try different stitches until you find the one that gives you the texture you want. It may be that in trying out stitches you change your idea slightly to a different yarn, so make up your mind completely before you have a quantity set aside.

Do keep to your original idea unless you change it for something you feel is better. An idea for a sweater may start as a classic but becomes something of a 'mongrel' if you try to put all your ideas together in one garment.

If the ideas are really so good they will wait until the next garment quite happily.

Once you have actually got a swatch of the stitch you want knitted, on needles that give the right sort of texture in the yarn you intend to use, you are ready to get down to work.

Just one point – when choosing the yarn do make certain that it suits the type of garment and your level of knitting skill. Not many people can successfully wear a shimmering Lurex garment for playing golf and it is quite hard work turning baby wool into a car coat.

The other yarns may fascinate you and you can be longing to use them, but they are safe in the shop until you are ready to design specially for them.

Getting Down to Facts

Decide from the swatch how many stitches and rows there are to the inch. It is a great pity to put a lot of work into something that is no use . . . at least for its original purpose.

From the very start, this is the way that ensures success, if for no other reason than that you take the trouble to measure correctly and make decisions in advance.

The simplest way is to plot what you intend to knit on a sheet of graph paper. Then already you have information that needs to be set down.

In one corner of the sheet of graph paper write down the number of stitches and rows to the inch from your swatch and the number of needles you used and the type of yarn chosen.

Beside this write down the measurements you require.

These measurements around the person will be taken with a measuring tape, but put it away when you are finished. The garment as it grows must be measured with a rigid ruler.

From now on you are going to 'map out' everything that is to be knitted. You are going to make a map of what the stitches are going to have to do, to make the design you want. You are going to map whether they are going to start as ribbing, how long you are going to work in pattern, and if the neck is going to divide and become a V-shaped neck.

Even the buttonholes should be marked out.

This is the moment to remember again that stitches are not square. You can plot and plan where every stitch goes but it is a plan, not an ordnance map to scale. This also means that it is not a paper pattern. When you are working in thick yarn with perhaps 4 stitches and 5 rows to the inch your plan of even a car coat may be quite small, but when you come to plan a lacy christening robe with perhaps 9 stitches and 14 rows to the inch you may even need to join two sheets of graph paper together.

Measurements

You will have noted down the measurements required, but if you noted them down directly from measuring someone with an inch tape you will have not yet considered whether this is wide enough for a sweater.

Tolerance.   Good though you may be about to prove yourself at this business of designing, no one can knit a second skin.

'Tolerance' is the name given for the variable amount added to basic measurements to give a garment 'ease' or final shaping. The result can sometimes be a more unusual, and eyecatching article. Not if the added width simply sags, however.

Tolerance differs from one type of garment to another. An evening sweater may be best with a small amount so that it fits tightly, an afternoon sweater may want a little more so that you can wear a fine blouse under it, and a sweater for sport will require more for freedom of movement and so that you can move easily and possibly cover a thinner pullover as well.

Planning a Sweater

As an example let us plan a sweater in double knitting, worked in stocking stitch for a 34 inch bust.

When you measured the tension it was 6 stitches and 8 rows to one inch and you worked the swatch you liked best on No 8 needles.

All this will be noted on the corner of your sheet.

To begin with it will be best to make a complete plan of the back, front and sleeves. Later you will find it is enough to make a plan of half of each. This is, of course, where the other half is identical.

When you measured you did not take into consideration additional tolerance for ease of wear.

As you are only planning the back of the sweater, you are only concerned with half of the 34 inches, which is 17 inches.

The total tolerance on a sweater could be 2 inches or it might be more. In this instance we will say 2 inches. As we are going to plan only the back we shall have to add only half of that amount.

When the width is 17 inches and there are 6 stitches to every inch that means 102 stitches to which must be added another 6 for tolerance. One thing more. At each side the sweater will be seamed and this will use two stitches from the back, one from each side. Rather than make the garment too tight it is better to add on to the total of 108 another 2 thus getting 110.

What Happens when you use Patterns

Stocking stitch was chosen for this first sweater, but it might have been a pattern where the repeat was 7 stitches and 1 extra stitch was required by the pattern.

This would not divide into 110. It could divide into 113 or 106 and you would have to decide whether you could lose just a little of the width or whether it would be better to use the larger number. Because it is a sweater, in this case I would have chosen the larger number.

Beginning to Chart

Let us assume for the time being that the sides of the sweater are going to be straight.

You must also make up your mind whether it is going to begin with rib or hem.

Whatever you choose, mark out the number of stitches you are going to cast on.

It is very easy to work in the future, if you decide on a few simple signs that will tell you what you want the stitch to do in that square. For instance I use / to show where a stitch is to be purled and the reverse slant for a knit stitch. When charting stocking stitch I only mark row ends because the entire row is bound to be the same, unless the work has to be increased or decreased and I use a small circle to show where a stitch is to be cast off.

Mark out the number of stitches to be cast on and also how the rib or welt is to be worked and how deep it is to be.

Subtract this depth from the total length to underarm. Suppose the answer is 12 inches. Then 12 inches have to be worked in stocking stitch and you can arrive at how many rows this is by multiplying 12 by 8, the number of rows to 1 inch. The answer is 96 and you can mark the graph paper 96 rows up so that you can see how the armholes are to be planned.

Once you are experienced it is not necessary to mark out so many rows of straight work. If this sweater was to be shaped in to the waist and brought out again just below the armhole line then it would be easy to mark on the decreases and increases and the number of rows apart you want them to be.

Planning Armholes

Measuring across between the points at which you intend the sleeves to join the main section will tell you how many stitches you want to lose for the armholes.

You have 113 stitches at the moment. If you want the sweater to measure 14 inches $2\frac{1}{2}$ inches above the start of the armhole shaping, then you will have 20 rows in which to cast off or decrease 26 or 28 stitches. Remember that again one stitch at either side will be lost in the armhole seam.

14 inches multiplied by 6 gives 84, plus 2 seam stitches which brings it to 86, but you have an odd number of stitches so you must make it either 85 or 87.

Say you choose to make it 87 then there are 26 stitches to use for armhole shaping, 13 at either side.

Armholes need to be a good curve so arrange this on the graph paper.

At each side you might cast off 4 stitches and then decrease one stitch at each end of the next two rows. You would now have reduced 12 of the 26 stitches.

To make the curve become a little more steep you might then decrease one stitch at each end of the next and every following alternate or right-side row until 11 stitches at each side had been decreased and finish off by making the next 2 decreases 4 rows apart.

Whatever you decided to do you must mark it down.

Measuring Length or Depth

Where you want to measure how long to make a side seam of

skirt or bodice or how deep to make an armhole you must measure directly. By this you lay the work flat and to measure the depth of an armhole you measure from the row where the armhole began straight up a line of stitches until the work is as long as required. You will get the wrong measurement if you try to go round the curve of the armhole.

Placing the Shoulder

The armhole depth is the next landmark and is measured from the beginning of the armhole including the rows of armhole shaping.

Mark the top edge lightly on the graph paper and then decide how wide the shoulders are to be.

Four inches wide will mean that each shoulder will need 24 stitches cast off for it. Shoulders are seldom straight but are slanting. This is obtained by casting the stitches off in groups at the beginning of several rows.

You might decide to have each shoulder in 6 groups of 4 stitches or 4 groups of 5 and 1 group of 4.

This would be worked for the first example by casting off 4 stitches at the beginning of the next and following 11 rows. When you have divided the work for a neck or opening and have only one shoulder on the needles at one time, you should cast off at the beginning of alternate rows, so that each cast-off group comes at the armhole edge of the work.

Sizes

It is not possible to give details of everything you may think of doing but there are a few books which can help you. Details of these are given on page 91. Sizes are best worked to the person's own measurements. If this is not always possible then the British Standard Measurements may be a guide.

One way of learning is to read and chart pattern instructions that you already have as leaflets or in magazines.

Although bust and chest sizes usually go up in 2 inch steps you will find that armholes may only lengthen by $\frac{1}{4}$ inch per size and shoulder seams grow wide even more gradually.

Make haste slowly and then you will at least make progress. Think before you mark anything on your chart and do remember that you have to be able to get into garments, that buttonholes may be required, and that if you really have an idea worth using there must be a way to knit it.

Perhaps you need to use the stitch downwards instead of upwards. No this is not silly. Skirts knitted downwards are very easy to fit because it is simple to stop when it is the right length for you.

Children's sweaters are ideal worked in this way because they can easily be lengthened as the child grows.

When you want something different knit it sideways, starting at the side edge and working across. A well-known stitch can look quite different this way up.

Take care with your measurements, try swatches out beforehand, plot each step and nothing is beyond your reach.

14. Overcoming Errors

In every craft, however carefully you work, mistakes do occur. Sometimes by far the best method is to admit they are wrong, unravel the knitting, steam the wool free of kinks and unevenness, rewind the wool and start all over again. There are occasions that are dealt with more easily and with considerably greater speed by rendering 'first aid', and it is these that are dealt with in this chapter.

Steaming Wool Smooth

Wool that has been unpicked, either from a newly knitted piece of garment or from an older, worn sweater that is going to be re-knitted, can be made smooth and easy to re-use by steaming. Do try a short length ONLY if you are uncertain as to whether the yarn is actually wool or if it is man-made fibre. Wool will take the heat of steam, whereas the man-made yarn may not.

Ideally the wool should be wound on to a skein holder, but it can also be wound round the framework of a clothes airer or an unvarnished chair back provided the strands are reasonably open to allow the circulation of steam. They should not all be piled tightly on top of each other.

Place the jet of steam from a large bowl of hot water or kettle so that the dampness of the steam covers the entire area of wool. Leave this for a few minutes for the steam to work and then leave the wool as it is until it is completely dry. When dry rewind into balls ready for use.

Dropped Stitches

The most common error even for the experienced knitter, is to accidentally pull the needles out of the work so dropping all the stitches or, at best, a large part of them. Picking up stitches either in a large quantity or in only one or two stitches can be tricky, but can be made easier if you go the right way about the job.

Picking up Many Stitches

Try to move the dropped stitches as little as possible, so that the matter does not become worse. Use a needle many sizes smaller than the one that the knitting has been on so that it will slip through the loops with the least disturbance. Get the loops on to the needle without considering whether some may have dropped further than others. Once they are all securely on the needle you can consider just how many may have gone further.

Should you find that one or more have been missed because they unravelled more quickly, anchor them by inserting a small safety pin or a loop of coloured thread. Using the correct size of needle take back one or more rows until all the stitches are on the same row.

Picking up a Few Dropped Stitches

When only a single stitch or one or two stitches have been dropped it is not necessary to take back the whole row. If you are not ready to deal with it immediately hold it from running further by placing a safety pin in it or a spare needle or loop of thread.

Once you are ready to attend to it insert the tip of the needle into it and the first or lowest strand of thread forming the 'ladder' above the actual loop. On stocking stitch with the knit side facing, the loop is simply lifted over the strand and dropped off the tip of the needle, the strand becoming the new stitch. If the stitch is several rows down, this process is repeated until it is worked up to the correct level.

On purl fabric work the stitch up on the wrong side as it is more difficult to bring the loop up through the purl stitch than it is on the knit side.

Some knitters prefer to use a small crochet hook to work the loop up the ladder of strands, and it may be that this does save you from possibly dropping another stitch off the tip of the needle.

Aim at doing the work correctly first time, but if you know you have made a mistake, take the trouble to correct it rather than hoping it will not show when the work is finished.

There are ways of camouflaging work if there is no other method of putting matters right.

Fault	Treatment
Too short	Whenever a garment or piece of work is the correct width, but is too short, it is possible to pick up stitches along the lower edge and work an extra strip downwards. On a sweater this might be worked as additional ribbing in a contrast colour.
Too long	Short amounts can be turned up as a hem. On sleeves the hem may be drawn tight to the wrist by the insertion of elastic through it.
	When a large amount has to be turned up it can be very bulky and is better removed. For this draw the thread right along one row tight towards the end of the row. Cut the thread, ease out the last few stitches and the amount you do not require will drop off. A small amount of the unwanted yarn can be unravelled and used to pick up the loops that are left, either to work a small hem on, a ribbed edge or just to cast them off.
Too large	Where a garment is too large it can be made smaller by re-seaming and cutting off the surplus knitting. This is not necessarily easy, particularly on thicker loosely knitted fabrics, and great care must be taken to anchor all the raw ends left by cutting. One of the simplest ways of doing this is to work a row of back-stitching or fine machine stitching all round each piece just outside the cutting line.
Too narrow	This is perhaps the most difficult problem to overcome. On a jacket or cardigan the only method is to take off the front bands and replace with wider edgings, or if it is without bands, to pick up stitches along the front edge and knit a strip on.
Elbows worn	Whether they are worn or badly darned they can be hidden by neat square knitted patches

Fault	*Treatment*
	or by suede or leather patches which promptly give it an expensive 'meant' look instead of appearing to be a renovation.
Hole	A small hole can become the starting point for an intentional pattern of small contrast coloured geometric patches or larger circular or star-shaped motifs.
Small mark or wrong stitch	A small mark can be covered by embroidery, a well placed initial if the mark comes in the right place or it may be covered by adding a few embroidered flower shapes or small motifs in Swiss darning.
Ridge of wrong dye lot	Depending on the position, it may be disguised by turning it into a yoke line by the addition of a row of embroidery. If it is in a more awkward position it may be necessary to work lines or even checks across the entire surface to cause it to be hidden.

Further Reading

Abbey, Barbara, *The Complete Book of Knitting*, Thames and Hudson, 1972.

Biggs, Diana, *Knitting: Stitches and Pattern*, Octopus, 1973.

Bray, Natalie, *Dress Pattern Designing*, Crosby Lockwood, 1970.

Bray, Natalie, *More Dress Pattern Designing*, Crosby Lockwood, 1970.

(The last two books are of particular use to would-be designers who wish to study how fashion trends are created from basic shapes.)

Collins, Marjorie, *Knitting*, Pelham Books, 1973.

Horne, Patience, and Bowden, Stephen, *Patons Book of Knitting and Crochet*, Heinemann, 1973.

Kiewe, Heinz Edgar, *The Sacred Book of Knitting*, 2nd edition, Art Needlework Industries Ltd, 1971.

Norbury, James, *Knit with James Norbury*, BBC 1968.

Phillips, Mary Walker, *Creative Knitting*, Van Nostrand Reinhold Co Ltd, 1972.

Thomas, Mary, *Knitting Book*, Hodder and Stoughton, 1972.

Thomas, Mary, *Book of Knitting Patterns*, Hodder and Stoughton, 1972.

Thompson, Gladys, *Guernsey and Jersey Patterns*, Batsford Ltd, 1969.

Walker, Barbara, *A Treasury of Knitting Patterns*, Sir Isaac Pitman and Sons Ltd, 1968.

Walker, Barbara, *A Second Treasury of Knitting Patterns*, Sir Isaac Pitman and Sons, Ltd, 1971.

(Both the above books are of great interest to any knitter looking for new stitches and unusual ideas.)

Kinmond, Jean, Ed, *Anchor Book of Lace Crafts*, Batsford Ltd, 1961.

Encyclopedia of Knitting, Odhams, 1968.

'Golden Hands' Encyclopedia of Knitting, Marshall Cavendish Ltd, 1973.

Knitting and Crochet Patterns in the 1920s, '30s and 40's, Duckworth, 1972.

Vogue Guide to Knitting, Collins, 1972.

Old Hand Knitters of the Dales, Dalesman, 1969.

Magazines which specialize in knitting patterns:

Family Circle
Golden Hands Monthly
Knitting and Sewing
Living
Mon Tricot (collections including 1030 Stitches and Patterns)
Pins and Needles
Woman
Woman and Home
Woman's Own
Woman's Weekly
Stitchcraft

Spinners' Addresses

All spinners are usually glad to be of advice in case of difficulty in obtaining yarns. They will also answer queries about their product which your usual stockist cannot deal with.

Emu, Emu Wools, Low Street, Keighley, Yorks BD21 5JD.

Hayfield, John C. Horsfall and Sons Ltd, Hayfield Mills, Glusburn, Nr Keighley, Yorks, BD20 8QP.

Jaeger, Jaeger Hand Knitting, PO Box 5, Suttington Road, Shepshed, Loughborough, Leics, LE12 5BR.

Ladyship, Baldwin and Walker, Westcroft Mills, Halifax, Yorks.

Lee Target, George Lee and Sons, PO Box 37, Wakefield Yorks.

Lister, Lister and Co, PO Box 37, Providence Mills, Wakefield, Yorks.

Mahoney, Martin Mahoney (GB), Coal Road, Seacroft, Leeds, Yorks LS14 2AQ.

Munrospun, Galashiels, Selkirk.

Patons, Patons and Baldwins (Sales), PO Box 22, Darlington, Co Durham.

Pingouin, French Wools Ltd, Lexington Street, London W1R 4BJ.

Robin, Robert Glew and Co, Roman Mills, Idle, Bradford BD10 9TE.

Sirdar, Sirdar, PO Box 31, Bective Mills, Alverthorpe, Wakefield, Yorks.

Templeton, John Templeton and Son Ltd, Worsted Mill, Ayr, Scotland.

Twilley, H. G. Twilley, Roman Mills, Stamford, Lincs PE9 1BG.

Wendy, Carter and Parker, Gordon Mills, Netherfield Road, Guisley, Yorks LS20 9PD.

Many yarns and knitting accessories are available, and a catalogue is available from:

The Needlewoman Shop, 146, Regent Street, London W1.

Standard Yarn Tensions

Tension Chart

Yarns knit to different tensions depending on the needles they are knitted on, the tightness with which you knit and the thickness of the yarn. This chart shows how different makes of yarn worked by the same knitter vary, and may act as a guide if you find that certain yarns are unobtainable and it is necessary to substitute a different yarn.

Basic yarn tension   *Types of yarn*
measured over 4 ins
(10cms) of stocking
stitch

30 sts and 36 rows on No 10 needles.	Emu. All 4 ply yarns.
	Sirdar. All 4 ply yarns.
30 sts and 40 rows on No 10 needles.	Twilley's Lysbet, Lyscordet and Goldfingering.
	Wendy, Invitation crochet cotton.
	Lister, Lavenda 3 ply.
28 sts and 36 rows on No 10 needles.	Twilley's Cortina.
	Lee Target, all 4 ply yarns.
	Lister, all 4 ply yarns.
	Robin, all 4 ply yarns.
	Hayfield, all 4 ply yarns.
	Patons, all 4 ply yarns.
	Wendy, Marriner.
28 sts and 40 rows on No 10 needles.	Twilley's Crysette.
24 sts and 32 rows on No 8 needles.	Robin, double knitting.
	Sirdar, double knitting.
	Wendy, double knitting nylonized.
22 sts and 28 rows on No 8 needles.	Lee Target, double knitting.
	Lister, double knitting.
	Hayfield, double knitting.
22 sts and 30 rows on No 8 needles.	Wendy Peter Pan Courtelle.
	Patons, double knitting.
22 sts and 32 rows on No 8 needles.	Emu, double knitting.

Standard Measurements

Standard Measurements

These measurements are only an approximate guide. There can be no better way of checking measurements before you design a garment than by measuring the individual it is intended for. These measurements may however help. Tolerance has not been added so allowances both for seams and for the degree of additional looseness required by the fashion and type of garment you intend to make must be added before you can accept the measurements as being the ones you are working to.

Babies and Toddlers

Approx age		0–3 months	3–6 months	6–12 months	1 yr	2 yr	3 yr
Chest	ins	18	19	20	21	22	23
Sleeve seam	ins	5½	5¾	6	6½	7¼	8¼
Wrist	ins	6	6⅛	6¼	6⅜	6½	6⅝
Upper arm	ins	7	7¼	7½	7¾	8	8¼
Shoulder seam	ins	2¼	2⅜	2½	2¾	3	3⅛
Width across back (between armholes)	ins	7¾	8	8¼	8½	8¾	9

Children

Chest	ins	24	26	28	30	32
Sleeve seam	ins	9½	11	12½	14	15
Wrist	ins	6¾	7	7	7¼	7½
Upper arm	ins	9	9¼	9½	9¾	10
Shoulder seam	ins	3¼	3½	3⅝	3¾	3⅞
Width across back (between armholes)	ins	10	10½	11	11¾	12¼

Women

Bust	ins	32	34	36	38	40	42	44
Sleeve seam	ins	16	16	16½	16½	17	17	17½
Wrist	ins	7½	7¾	8¼	8¾	9	9¼	9½
Upper arm	ins	11	11½	12	12½	13	13½	14
Shoulder seam	ins	3⅞	4	4⅛	4¾	4½	4⅝	4¾
Width across back between armholes	ins	13¾	14	14¼	14½	14¾	15	15¼

Men

Chest	ins	36	38	40	42	44	46	48
Sleeve seam	ins	17	17½	18	18½	18¾	19	19¼
Wrist	ins	9½	10	10½	11	11½	12	12½
Upper arm	ins	13½	13¾	14	14¼	14½	15	15½
Shoulder seam	ins	4⅜	4½	4⅝	4¾	5	5¼	5⅜
Width across back (between armholes)	ins	15	15¼	15½	15¾	16	16¼	16½

Index